PRESERVING FIELD RECORDS

PRESERVING FIELD RECORDS
Archival Techniques
for Archaeologists and Anthropologists

Mary Anne Kenworthy
Eleanor M. King
Mary Elizabeth Ruwell
Trudy Van Houten

Published by   1985
THE UNIVERSITY MUSEUM
University of Pennsylvania

Design, editing, production
Publications Division, The University Museum

Typesetting
The Sheridan Press, Hanover, Pennsylvania

Printing
Cushing-Malloy, Inc., Ann Arbor, Michigan

Library of Congress Cataloging-in-Publication Data
Main entry under title:

Preserving field records.
 Bibliography: p.
 1. Anthropological archives—Management.
2. Archaeological archives—Management. 3. Archives—
Management. I. Kenworthy, Mary Anne. II. University
of Pennsylvania. University Museum.
GN14.P74 1985 069.5 85-21007
ISBN 0-934718-72-5

TABLE OF CONTENTS

ACKNOWLEDGMENTS

The manual could not have been completed without the assistance of a number of people at various stages of the project. The manual staff benefited from comments by the following readers and reviewers of different sections of the text: members of the Conservation Center for Art and Historic Artifacts, Bruce Ambacher, Nicholas Hartmann, John Hastings, and Debbie Hess Norris. Valuable help in locating photographs was provided by Kathleen Baxter, Douglas Craig, Caroline Dosker, Robert Harding, Kenneth Hazell, Lee Horne, Francis E. Johnston, Ruth Leiby, Bryce Little, Edward O'Driscoll, Mark Philbrick, Barbara and Fred Roll, Joan Schall, Fred Schoch, Robert Sharer, David Stephen, John Taggart, Arthur Vokes, and Joyce White. The expertise of The University Museum Publication Department guided us through the perils of printers and proofs: Barbara Hayden, Barbara Murray, Martha Phillips, Jennifer Quick, Raymond Rorke, and Karen Vellucci. Finally, William Baden, Georgianna Grentzenberg, John Hastings, and Katherine Moreau gave us special assistance and moral support in our times of greatest need. We would like to thank everyone who helped in the successful completion of this project.

M.A.K.
E.M.K.
M.E.R.
T.V.H.

PREFACE

The manual that follows was prepared by the staff of the University Museum Archives, where a systematic program of document accession and storage has been carried out since 1981. The Archives was established when the Museum realized that its older field records were deteriorating, were difficult to use, and that proper storage of documents being generated by current projects also presented a problem. The establishment of the Archives in the former Elkins Library allowed the existing records to be collected and organized, and in 1984 a *Guide to The University Museum Archives* was prepared to help publicize their contents. The Archives now serves as a resource for scholars studying the history of the anthropological and archaeological research conducted by The University Museum, and the collections that resulted from these activities over the past century.

The process of creating the Archives revealed that most field researchers lack a basic knowledge of the archival principles and techniques that contribute to record longevity. The idea of writing an introductory manual on this subject was thus born. The National Historic Publications and Records Commission (National Archives and Records Administration) supplied funding to bring together the professional expertise necessary for a comprehensive project. The University Museum presented the concept to national organizations involved in archaeology, anthropology, and archives. The need for such a manual was immediately recognized. Representatives of these institutions served on an Advisory Committee, which oversaw the various drafts written by Museum Archives staff members. The cooperation and enthusiasm demonstrated by the various participants has been encouraging, and I wish to take this opportunity to thank all of them for their contributions in making this publication possible.

Robert H. Dyson, Jr.,
Director
The University Museum

Advisory Committee

American Anthropological Association   Stephen Williams
Peabody Museum

American Philosophical Society   Stephen Catlett

National Anthropological Archives, Smithsonian Institution   James Glenn

Archaeological Institute of America   Jane Ayer Scott
Harvard University

Society for American Archaeology   William Rathje
University of Arizona

Society of American Archivists   John Baker
New York Public Library

Society for Historical Archaeology   Stephanie Rodeffer
National Park Service

The University Museum   Robert H. Dyson, Jr.
Mary Anne Kenworthy
Eleanor King
Mary Elizabeth Ruwell
Leslie Simon
Trudy Van Houten

Surveying at Tepe Hissar, Iran, 1931. The site was originally excavated by Erich Schmidt from 1931–1933. The field records, now housed in The University Museum Archives, were used extensively by members of the expedition that re-excavated the site in 1976 under the direction of Robert H. Dyson, Jr., and Maurizio Tosi. (The University Museum, University of Pennsylvania)

INTRODUCTION

Mary Elizabeth Ruwell

Imagine yourself at a site or in a village where someone else worked fifty years ago. If you are lucky, the person or institution sponsoring the project will have thought to store the records where you can find them. Unfortunately, locating the material may only be the beginning of your difficulties. You may find correspondence, but not the actual fieldnotes. Or you may find exactly the records you need only to realize that you cannot read any of the material. The papers are moldy and the ink has faded. The color photographs have turned into blank white squares. The machine-readable records were created using unknown hardware and software, and you cannot find out what they contain. You may already have encountered this situation in the course of your own research. It could also happen to someone else looking for your field records in fifty years.

This short manual is intended for archaeologists and anthropologists who are interested in materials and techniques that will greatly prolong the useful life of their field records. Archaeological and anthropological research generates primary source material that can never be duplicated. Excavations disturb remains that have lain intact for centuries. Similarly, contact with a foreign anthropologist may change the culture being studied. Even fieldnotes of published expeditions may contain evidence whose importance may not have been understood initially, but which may later prove vital to the further advance of knowledge. Once fieldwork is completed, only photographs and written or taped documentation remain to reconstruct the subject of research as it was originally. It is of paramount importance, therefore, that these records themselves be made as durable as possible.

Field records must also be properly organized and preserved if their future research potential is to be realized. Archaeological and anthropological records require a higher percentage of reten-

William Schauffler of the Ban Chiang Project counting sherd bags, 1976. Ban Chiang, like other modern projects, generated a huge amount of data that required both sophisticated new methods of analysis and vastly increased documentation. (Courtesy of the Ban Chiang Project, The University Museum, University of Pennsylvania)

tion than do many other types of records. Only five percent of all office records, for example, should be considered for archival retention. Field records, on the other hand, are scientific experiments for which nearly all of the available documentation is pertinent.

Recent developments in field methodology accentuate this need. Field documentation has become progressively more systematic and, as a consequence, vastly more voluminous. The increase is dramatic. The National Anthropological Archives of the Smithsonian Institution contains records from surveys of Native American sites over wide geographic areas. The Bureau of American Ethnology conducted a Mound Survey from 1881 to 1889 that produced about five linear feet of material. The River Basin Surveys, a salvage archaeology project conducted from 1947 to 1969, produced about 370 linear feet of permanent records. Because of the abundance of material, publications are increasingly emphasizing summaries and interpretations of findings. The field records must be retained and made accessible, however, as they are the only database for continued research.

Despite the care and diligence with which researchers collect their data, they are often recorded on highly impermanent media. Inattention to paper, film, or ink qualities, for instance, may lead to serious problems of deterioration over the years. Records, even those stored carefully, have become irretrievably damaged or barely salvageable because of the type and quality of material used. Today, yellow carbon copies from the 1930s will disintegrate in your hands and photostatic copies from the 1950s contain only vague outlines of a printed page.

This manual is a collaborative effort between anthropologists and archivists to help prevent scientific losses in the future by presenting archival techniques for researchers who are currently generating records. By knowing the standards for archival quality documentation, the fieldworker will be able to choose materials and processes best able to guarantee maximum longevity. It seems clear that in some cases there is no one solution. Priorities vary. In many cases, archival principles and methods can only partially be adapted to field conditions. Certain materials may be more appropriate in one geographical location than in another. The manual attempts to provide guidelines and possible solutions rather than rigid specifications. Professional anthropologists and archaeologists know the documentation required by their re-

This drawing of an Egyptian column was recorded on acidic paper that became stained and brittle with age before it was encapsulated for protection against further mechanical damage (see Chapter 2). (The University Museum, University of Pennsylvania)

search. The aim of this publication is to help them make certain that information is recorded and stored in the best way available.

The use of archival materials and techniques does not always entail a greater cost for the researcher or project. The quality of paper, for instance, is not always related to the price. In the long run, the products recommended in this manual may save the researcher money. It is also important to think about the records beforehand and allow for preventive or remedial measures of record preservation in developing project budgets. If film must be quickly processed on site, it may be necessary to allow funds for recopying some of those photographs later, using laboratory processes that guarantee important images will be as stable as possible. Advance planning will ensure that funds for preservation are there when they are needed.

The first chapter of this manual is a survey of existing field documentation, addressing the types of records generated by research and the need to identify those records worthy of special attention. Subsequent chapters provide technical explanations of the quality of papers, film, tape, and other recording media. Each medium has different characteristics that must be considered in making it permanent and durable. The destructive effects of acid, the enemy that rapidly turns old newspaper yellow, recurs as a common theme. Machine-readable records represent a special challenge since new products are introduced almost daily. The final chapter on storage explains what can be done to store field records safely in offices or other interim locations, and also describes long-term archival storage.

A bibliography for each chapter is provided at the end of the manual. The manual is not intended to be a technical treatise, but rather is aimed at providing the basic knowledge necessary for making decisions about record preservation. A list of manufacturers offering archival materials and supplies can be found in the pocket on the back cover. The University Museum Archives will furnish updated lists in the future at a nominal charge. We welcome comments, suggestions, and questions.

Additional advice on organizing and preserving field records should be sought from the repository where project records will eventually reside. A few institutions, among the best-known of which are the National Anthropological Archives of the Smithsonian Institution and the American Philosophical Society, encourage donation of field research. In addition, many museums

Julian Steward with a Shoshonean informant in the 1930s. Field photographs are among the records preserved by the National Anthropological Archives of the Smithsonian Institution. (Courtesy of the Smithsonian Institution)

and research centers offer facilities for storage of field project records. These repositories will gladly furnish guidelines for record transfer and will explain record use policies and restrictions. The manual Advisory Committee encourages field directors to anticipate these requirements. The more care given to records as they are generated, the fewer the problems that will occur with their future storage and accessibility.

CHAPTER 1. FORMATS OF ANTHROPOLOGICAL AND ARCHAEOLOGICAL RECORDS

Eleanor M. King

Recommendations

- Assess the archival importance of a project at its inception.

- Determine which specific documents, generated at different stages of research, will have the greatest future value. Re-evaluate your decisions as the project develops.

- Select the most suitable supplies for critical documents in the budgetary stage of planning.

- Budget for preservation activities as an integral part of the project.

- Label all field notebooks, drawings and other records, and document how records are created.

- Keep important records in one place and use in/out cards or other controls when they are loaned or taken elsewhere.

- Purchase reference booklets on proper archival procedures and standards at the start of the project from the American National Standards Institute (ANSI) or other sources listed in the bibliography.

Survey of Project Documentation

To assess the physical format of the records kept by anthropologists, we conducted an informal survey of expedition records housed in The University Museum Archives and documents retained by on-going field projects within the Museum and other institutions. Our goal was to see what kinds of supplies—paper, film, tape, disks—were most frequently used so we could make appropriate recommendations for record preservation. We also wanted to know how researchers viewed their own projects, particularly what were considered the most important records, and what steps were taken to ensure preservation. We intended to cover procedures and supplies in the manual that were generally known and to suggest specific alternatives to current practices.

The four anthropological subfields of physical anthropology, ethnography, linguistics, and archaeology were all represented in our survey, as well as classical archaeology and Egyptology. A corresponding variety of research activities also were considered, including observation, interviewing, excavation, survey, documentary research, and laboratory analysis. A wide range of geographic areas was likewise sought, so we could gauge the effect of different climates and local supply situations on anthropological record-keeping.

Not surprisingly, we found substantial variety in the preferred methods of documentation. The types of records generated, however, can loosely be grouped into general categories reflecting the separate stages of a typical project. These stages underscore the fact that, although fieldwork frequently generates the bulk of the records, it does not comprise the only documentation for such research. Materials produced by preparatory work, post-field analysis, and publication are also part of the record. How critical the documents from each stage are depends on the type of project and the assessment of the researcher. These criteria will be discussed in detail below.

Documents from the planning stage of a typical project often contain crucial information not repeated elsewhere. Proposals, correspondence, and similar records give the original reasons for research in an area or on a particular topic. On-site reconnaissance records such as annotated commercial maps showing the location of archaeological sites or the distribution of various ethnic groups can be invaluable documents, particularly when subsequent research is confined to just one site or group of people. The value of planning information can be measured directly by the extent to which it is repeated in other records. A research publication, for example, might give all the historical data on a project and its inception, thereby diminishing the

Robert S. O. Harding observing a baboon in Gilgil, Kenya, 1976. Each type of anthropological/archaeological research has its own methods of documentation, and produces a unique set of essential records. (Courtesy of R. Harding, Department of Anthropology, University of Pennsylvania)

importance of the documents from which the account was developed. Most of these overviews are subjective and selective, however, and the unpublished information may reveal other important perspectives.

Fieldwork records, on the other hand, almost always have primary significance. They are the raw data on which analysis builds, and are critical not only to the project for which they are collected, but also subsequently, as other researchers attempt to further previous work. They are usually irreplaceable and unreconstructable if lost. Fieldwork documents can be separated into the two broad classes of data recording and project administration, with the first being the most important. Data records include documents such as fieldnotes, catalogues, plans, drawings, photographs, sound recordings, motion pictures, and machine-readable materials. Administrative records include correspondence, billing and shipping notices, and publicity bulletins. Correspondence can be particularly important in documenting how a project developed or why certain decisions were made.

Frank H. H. Roberts, Jr., plotting the distribution of bones and artifacts in the Folsom occupation level, Lindenmeier site, Colorado, in the 1930s. Fieldwork generates data that can be irreplaceable if lost. (Courtesy of the Smithsonian Institution)

The analysis stage generates its own share of information, which is as significant as the fieldwork data it synthesizes and interprets. Analytic records tend to be more easily reproduced than fieldwork documents, however, especially with the increasing use of computers for data manipulation. Documents from this stage of research include such items as tables, drawings, machine-readable data and special programs, printouts, indexed card files, manuscript reports, correspondence, billing records, and photographs. The relative importance of each of these materials in documenting research progress depends again on the information it conveys and whether it can be replicated without difficulty.

Publication, the final stage, usually produces the most readily available records, as they frequently exist in several copies. Opinions vary as to their archival utility. Some consider the publication stage to be the least important for documenting a project, since the final product is so widely distributed. Others feel, however, that changes made during the process have intrinsic value or

Chief Mountain Chief of the Blackfoot listening to the recording of a song and interpreting it in sign language for Frances Densmore in front of the Smithsonian, March 1916. Analysis of information is as critical as its collection. (Courtesy of the Smithsonian Institution)

historical significance. Certain researchers interviewed, for example, thought that final publication drawings were more important than field originals, because of the former's greater quality and durability. Records from this stage include manuscript drafts, proofs, machine-readable files, correspondence, photographic prints, and materials prepared for photography, such as inked drawings, plans, maps and tables, and offprints.

Each phase of a project generates a variety of physical types of record, from paper through machine-readable records, though the emphasis on one or another type may shift from stage to stage or project to project. Despite the range of documentation, the materials on which information is encoded do not vary that much. They can be segregated into a few major categories to assess durability and conservation. Paper records predominate, with the bulk being formed by notebooks (all sizes) and card files (all sizes). Also important are mimeographed, typed, photocopied, and handwritten loose-leaf sheets (usually 8.5 x 11 inches or 8.5 x 14 inches); graph paper, polyester film, vellum, and tracing paper (all sizes); and computer printouts. Photographic records are almost as extensive, with negatives, slides, and contact or other prints usually included (both black and white, and color). Becoming more prevalent are machine-readable records such as disks, computer cassettes, or magnetic tapes. Less common, but crucial for ethnographic and linguistic research, are reel-to-reel or cassette tapes and motion picture reels. Each of the major types of record will be discussed in separate chapters. Here we will concentrate on one of the most essential steps in preservation: document appraisal.

Evaluating Project Records

The total amount of a particular physical record a project generates depends on both subject matter and objectives. So too, the importance of specific records varies. A linguistic project, for example, might produce many cassette recordings that, along with their paper transcriptions, are the prime documentation for the fieldwork. An archaeological project, on the other hand, might emphasize photographs and drawings as vital excavation records. Different researchers also value the same type of physical records differently. Correspondence, for instance, is deemed expendable by some, whereas others, as noted above, find letters useful in

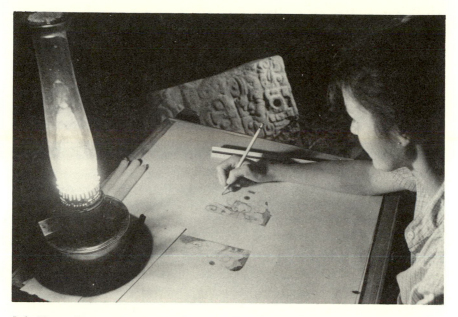

Jody Harper Hansen drawing a stela at the site of El Mirador, Guatemala, 1982. (Courtesy of Mark Philbrick, Brigham Young University Public Communications)

reconstructing the intellectual history of their project. Careful selection of which records to preserve permanently is necessary, as documents such as drawings can be redundant and storage space is often a serious practical consideration in offices as well as in archives. The cost of using only archivally approved materials for all records can also be prohibitive. Researchers therefore need to exercise judgment about which documents to preserve and which materials to use from the time of project inception through all stages to completion.

Unfortunately, many scholars do not see beyond their immediate research goals to the future reconstructability or archival importance of their projects. This lack of foresight is especially characteristic of younger researchers and of those who have never had to deal with archival records. For example, scholars working in areas of the world that have long-standing research traditions, like the Near East and Egypt, are the most likely to appreciate the importance of archival holdings and to be conscious of the archival importance of their own work, as they themselves have had to rely on earlier accounts.

The key to complete documentation is awareness. The researcher needs to keep the ultimate record in mind at every stage of the project, and to review periodically the accumulation of documentary material. The latter is particularly important as one's evaluation is not always consistent from inception to completion, with hindsight often enhancing the importance of one set of documents and/or diminishing the significance of another. One archaeologist polled, for instance, noted that color slides taken strictly for purposes of lecturing proved to reveal certain excavation details not included in the project's paper records or black and white photographs. From a subsidiary data set, the color slides thus became an integral part of the project record. Evaluation of documents should begin with project planning and should be renewed every step of the way so that a permanent record may be ensured.

Even when a careful appraisal has been made of which documents to preserve, problems may arise. Budgetary and other logistical considerations often make it imperative to rely on local products or processes of uncertain or uncontrollable quality. Shipping all the supplies for a large field expedition is often prohibitively expensive, for instance. Supplies may also run out during the course of the work. In either case, the researcher must make do with whatever materials are readily available, which may or may not be of good quality or amenable to long-term preservation. In other cases, a lengthy field season may necessitate reliance on local processes such as photocopying or film developing. Ektachrome, for example, is a widely distributed, easily processed color film that can be developed outside specialized labs. It is a favorite with many researchers who want immediate feedback on the quality of the pictures they have taken, or who simply need the photographs for their ongoing work. Unfortunately, however, Ektachrome is not stable, and its color deteriorates much faster than that of other films.

There are two remedies to this kind of problem. The first, as noted, is to make a careful appraisal right from the beginning of which documents are likely to be the most crucial, to select the best materials for those, and to continue re-evaluating that assessment as research proceeds. The second is to emphasize out-of-field conservation and storage. If the most suitable notebooks for recording observations are made of poor quality paper, they can still be used and then photocopied on archival paper with no loss of information. All records can be preserved. The crucial

Nunzio Lione, Giacinto Loisi, and Elizabeth Ralph making a cesium magnetometer survey of the site of Gravina, Italy, in the fall of 1965. Choice of which documents to preserve depends on the type of project and the information being sought. (The University Museum, University of Pennsylvania)

question is choosing which are more important and worthy of special attention, given the limitations of funding and storage space.

Both solutions require careful allocation of research funds, as both entail specific trade-offs. Fewer rolls of film purchased for use in the field, for example, may mean more money later for proper photographic storage. Similarly, having better on-site drawing supplies may prove to be more economical in the long run than copying original maps made on cheap paper. Such practical details should be thought out ahead of time, and the necessary costs for preservation incorporated into budget proposals from the start.

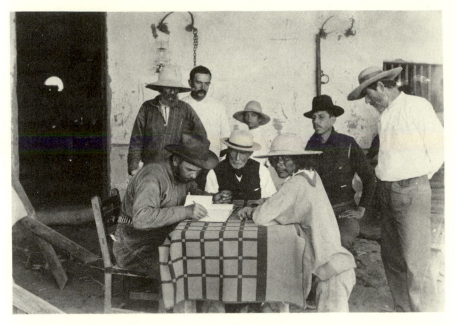

W. J. McGee collecting a vocabulary from subchief Mashem of the Seri (right foreground), Sonora, Mexico, 1894. Fieldnotes are often the most critical documentary sources. (Courtesy of the Smithsonian Institution)

Suggestions for Researchers

Planning in advance which records to keep for each phase of research is the most critical step the director(s) can take to ensure that a project is properly documented and can be reconstructed in the future. All too often, research records cover one stage of work but not another. Planning is also important in determining which physical materials to select for project records. If photographs are to be the main source of documentation, for example, researchers may choose to spend more on better quality film and storage containers than on paper for notes and correspondence.

Planning involves a number of procedures. At the time of the project's inception, the director(s) should evaluate its potential archival importance, that is, the likelihood of other researchers needing to refer to original records in the future. Research in new directions always has historical value; however, certain projects may require fuller documentation than others. Archaeological contract work, for example, which records cultural resources later destroyed by construction, needs to be particularly well documented to allow accurate reconstruction of the lost site(s).

For each stage of the project, the director(s) must select those documents that are the most critical. This choice depends both on personal views and on the assessment of future research interest. While it is not possible to predict what later scholars might be looking for, it is undoubtedly fair to assume that fieldnotes are more significant than bills, for instance, in documenting a project, and should receive greater attention for preservation. The extent to which the researcher can control the quality of a particular kind of document will greatly influence these decisions. Purchasing film is within a director's purview. Prescribing the type of paper to be used by correspondents is not. The best approach is obviously to emphasize preservation and safekeeping of those documents over which one has the greatest direct control. The highest quality materials should be used for the most important records.

Trade-offs in the allocation of funds should be gauged carefully before going to the field. If Ektachrome is used to allow photo processing *in situ* with funds from local sources, then money should be reserved for post-fieldwork conservation copying of selected images onto Kodachrome or black and white film. Project proposals should incorporate such considerations directly into their budgets. Otherwise, researchers back from the field may find themselves with deteriorating records and no means to preserve them.

Once the project starts, the director(s) should make sure that all the documentation is clear. Written material should be reasonably legible, drawings labelled, and field notebooks identified. Most important, information on how documents are created should be kept. For example, if a system of abbreviation is used, the director(s) should keep a key to it with the documents. All too often records remain inaccessible to other scholars because a perfectly simple method of shorthand notation is nowhere explained and can only be reconstructed after much work.

Important records should be stored as much as possible in one place and their removal controlled by the use of in/out cards or a comparable system. Dispersal or loss of crucial documentation is most likely to happen when no centralized record of its location is kept.

Finally, researchers are encouraged to refer throughout all project stages to American National Standards Institute (ANSI) booklets and to other literature listed in the manual's bibliography to become acquainted with archival standards and procedures. Many conservation problems can be solved before project documents ever reach an archives. Simple steps to ensure preservation as the project develops save time, effort, and repair costs when the records are eventually transferred to their final repository. Having some pertinent reference works on hand will encourage thoughtful decisions as problems occur.

CHAPTER 2. PRESERVATION OF PAPER RECORDS

Trudy Van Houten

Recommendations

• All paper field records should be typed, written, or photocopied *legibly*.

• Paper field records should be labelled to indicate site, date, author, and any other information essential for their identification. All pages should be numbered. Drafts should be labelled "rough" or "final".

• Only acid-free paper should be used for important field documents; alkaline reserve paper is even safer. Alternatively, ordinary paper can be used to record information that will be later photocopied on acid-free paper. Newly purchased acid-free paper should be tested with a pH testing pen to verify that its pH is 7 or higher.

• Paper records should be protected from acid migrating into them from low pH file folders, cardboard notebook covers, newsprint, and any other sources of acid. Only photocopies of newspaper clippings should be stored with important field records, and only acid-free folders and boxes should be used to store important files.

• Only heat-fusion photocopying processes should be used to copy important documents.

• Important papers should be protected from ultraviolet (UV) light. Sunlight and fluorescent tubes are major sources of UV light. In the field, paper records should be kept in the shade whenever possible; in the office, they should be boxed or filed.

• Paper records should be kept as cool as possible, and should be protected from fluctuations in temperature. They should not be kept in attics, cars, or against the outside walls of buildings for prolonged periods of time.

• Important paper records should be carefully humidified if the ambient relative humidity falls below 40%. Paper records are prone to mold and mildew growth and to foxing (red/brown staining) when the relative humidity exceeds 60%. In humid climates, measures should be taken to keep records dry. Dessicants, such as silica gel, can be placed in containers used to store paper records in humid environments. Fluctuations in humidity should be avoided whenever possible.

• Documents should be protected from hungry insects and rodents. Metal boxes generally prevent the incursions of these pests. Infested field documents should be fumigated *prior to shipping them back to the office or laboratory*. Orthophenyl phenol is probably the safest fumigation chemical.

• Paper records should be protected from environmental pollution due to car exhausts, cigarette smoke, and urban air as much as possible. They should be kept in closed containers to prevent their contamination by particulate matter (dirt, dust, ashes), and they should only be kept in environments with acceptably low levels of gaseous pollution. These precautions may extend the longevity of the author as well as of the records.

• Carbon typewriter ribbons and pencils are the most durable and safest writing media. Many inks are damaging or impermanent. Documents recorded using felt-tip or ballpoint pens should be photocopied for storage.

• Pressure-sensitive labels and tape should NEVER be used to mend paper records. Labelling, mending, fastening, or corrections achieved using pressure-sensitive materials do not last, and pressure-sensitive materials will permanently damage any papers to which they are applied. Use British Museum tape or vegetable starch paste and water for mending. Rubber cement is another dangerous adhesive, and it should not be used.

• Papers should be bent or folded as seldom as possible. They should not be permitted to sag or crumple in file folders.

• Steel paperclips and staples rust and destroy the edges of paper records to which they are affixed. Use inert plastic clips or stainless steel or aluminum staples instead.

• Use only soft cloth, eraser crumbs, gum or white vinyl erasers, or an archivists' cleaning pad to remove surface dirt from paper records. Work gently from the center outward, taking care not to damage the edges.

- Polyester folders or encapsulation will protect important documents from mechanical damage, dust, and dirt. This treatment is particularly useful for large paper records, such as site plans and maps, that are often subjected to rough conditions and hard use. Polyester folders can also be used to protect fragile or damaged documents.

- The restoration or cleaning of important original documents should be undertaken by professional paper conservators only.

Introduction

The documentation for many anthropological or archaeological research projects still consists largely, if not exclusively, of paper records. These records represent a crucial resource for contemporary scholars, and a valuable legacy for future ones. In this light, it is dismaying to consider how often paper records have proven unworthy of the important information entrusted to their fragile surfaces. Archivists are aware of many examples of field records rendered useless by illegible handwriting; lack of definite provenience; missing data, pages, or documents; or physical deterioration.

While paper field records will always be subject to damage and losses occasioned by the vicissitudes of travel, field conditions, and fate, many of the circumstances that imperil these documents can be prevented or mitigated. Care in ensuring that documents are legible, adequately identified, and complete will contribute substantially to their longevity. The physical deterioration of paper field records can also be prevented or considerably delayed. This chapter describes the chemical and physical factors that cause paper records to deteriorate, and the steps that can be taken to protect them.

Paper Permanence and Durability

Permanence is the ability of paper to remain chemically stable over time and to resist deterioration resulting from intrinsic factors,

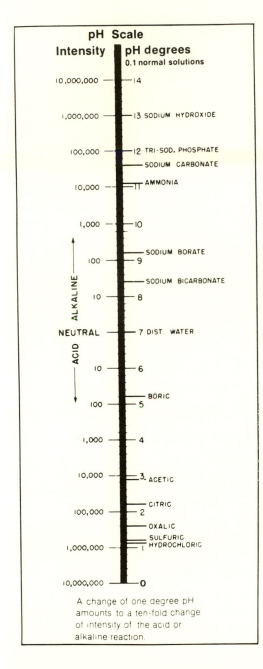

[pH scale] (From Keepers of Light by William Crawford, published by Morgan & Morgan, Dobbs Ferry, New York, 1979)

such as impurities in the paper itself, or extrinsic factors, such as environmental pollutants. Permanent papers resist discoloration and retain their original texture. The most permanent papers are acid-free or alkaline papers having a pH of 7 or more. Acidity is the chief agent of paper *im*permanence. Paper consists primarily of cellulose, a stable polysaccharide ($C_6H_{10}O_5$) that constitutes the chief part of plant cell walls. The acid in paper hydrolyzes or breaks down the cellulose molecules, severing the molecular bonds and splitting the molecules into shorter chains. Over time, acid causes paper to become stained, weak, and brittle.

Durability is the degree to which paper retains its original physical strength and mechanical properties over time, especially under conditions of heavy use. Durable papers resist tearing, fraying, or cracking. The most durable papers are made from long cotton or rag fibers, or from the long fibers of softwood (coniferous) trees which have been treated to remove naturally occurring plant acids. Papers made from long cellulose fibers have greater resistance to damage caused by folding and flexing than papers made from shorter cellulose fibers.

No paper is absolutely permanent and durable. Paper and other writing supplies are complex organic substances that inevitably deteriorate over time.

Factors that adversely affect paper permanence will also adversely affect paper durability. As the molecules within a cellulose fiber are hydrolyzed, the fibers themselves weaken and break. Oxidation also causes cellulose molecules to depolymerize, or split into shorter chains, and it too can weaken and break the cellulose fibers. Normally, oxidation is very gradual, taking place over hundreds of years. The inevitable process of oxidation can be accelerated, however, by the presence of ozone, a gaseous environmental pollutant, or by the peroxides produced by the acid reactions in paper. So the presence of acids and oxidants in paper adversely affects durability as well as permanence.

Papers may be durable but not permanent, or permanent but not durable. The paper used in telephone books must be durable, since telephone books are heavily used, but it need not be permanent since telephone books are only used for short periods of time. By contrast, the paper used for archival records must be permanent, since it must last for long periods of time, but it need not be durable, since archival records are seldom heavily used.

Encyclopedias and dictionaries are intended to be both permanent and durable (S. D. Warren Company 1981).

A Brief History of Papermaking

The first true paper is said to have been invented in China by T'sai Lun in approximately A. D. 105. Paper sizing, which improves the writing surface and reduces feathering or blurring of waterbased ink, was developed in China by approximately A. D. 700. Early sizings included gypsum, rice starch or flour, and lichen glue (Barrow 1974).

Papermaking technology reached Korea and Japan by approximately A. D 600. In A. D. 711, Chinese prisoners of war brought papermaking to Samarkand. From Samarkand, the technology spread throughout the Arab world. The Moorish invasion of Spain brought papermaking to Europe in A. D. 713 and by A. D. 1495, the technology had spread to every European country.

The steps involved in papermaking have changed little over the last 2,000 years, but the machines and chemical additives used at each step in the process have changed dramatically.

Paper can be made from almost any plant rich in cellulose. Papers have been made from hemp, rice, cotton, wasps' nests, mulberry leaves, artichokes, straw, seaweed, flax, and potatoes. The process of papermaking begins when plant fibers are macerated until they flatten and separate into tiny fabrilles. The fibers are then mixed with water and other materials and spread evenly across a screen to drain. As the cellulose fibers dry, they form a tight mesh: "The paper sheet is formed by mechanical entanglement of the fibers' fabrilles, chemical bonding of adjacent cellulose molecules (hydrogen bonding), surface tension between fibers, and adhesive action of nonfiber additives" (Ritzenthaler 1983).

Paper made prior to the seventeenth century is almost always both durable and permanent. It is durable because the cellulose fibers in early papers consist of very long fibers of cotton or flax from rags, and the processes used to macerate the rags were so gentle that the fibers were not broken. The rag fibers in early handmade papers were macerated in a mortar and pestle, moistened and allowed to decompose in the sun, or tenderized by mixing them with lime or milk. The addition of lime or milk increased the alkalinity of paper made from these rags since residual magnesium and calcium carbonates remained in the paper after the water had been drained off. Lime was also added to early paper as a filler and whitener.

The stamping mill, invented in the twelfth century, consisted of wooden beaters in a wooden tub. Use of the stamping mill allowed paper to be pulped faster without significantly shortening the fibers. After 1337, paper was hand-dipped in gelatin sizing to provide a better writing surface and to prevent waterbased ink from feathering. Gelatin is chemically neutral.

So the earliest papers were durable because they were made with long plant fibers and permanent because they were chemically somewhat alkaline. The printing of the Gutenberg Bible was completed in 1455, and by 1487, the need for paper far exceeded its supply. The history of papermaking after the invention of the printing press consists of a series of technological developments that permitted more paper to be produced faster in order to meet the increasingly urgent demand for it. This industrial expansion was achieved only at the expense of paper permanence and durability, however. The seventeenth and nineteenth centuries were periods of particularly rapid technological change in paper manufacture.

Intrinsic Enemies of Paper Records

In 1620, paper manufacturers began to add alum (potassium aluminate) to stabilize and preserve paper and to increase the effectiveness of its gelatin sizing. Unfortunately, alum is an acid salt that degrades to form sulphuric acid, increasing paper acidity and decreasing paper permanence.

The Hollander beater was invented in 1680 to macerate plant fibers more quickly. The Hollander beater consisted of a metal bed and a series of whirling metal plates. The Hollander beater greatly reduced the amount of time required to macerate and separate cellulose fibers, but it also reduced the length of the cellulose fibers produced and the durability of paper made from these shorter fibers. Another disadvantage of the Hollander beater was that small metallic particles were shed by the metal parts during the maceration process. These particles weakened and discolored the paper. The Hollander beater macerated rags so efficiently that they required no prior processing with lime or

Papermaking in the 17th century. (Original woodcut in Descriptions des arts et matières *by Jerome Joseph Lefrançois, Paris, 1761; courtesy of Lindenmeyr Paper Company)*

milk, so papers manufactured using the Hollander beater also tended to be less alkaline and less permanent.

Rags were first whitened with chlorine bleach in 1774. Chlorine bleach leaves an acid residue in paper if it is not completely rinsed out of the pulp. The Fourdrinier and cylinder papermaking machines, which heated the paper instead of allowing it to air dry, were invented during the nineteenth century, and the Jordan refiner, which produced even shorter fibers, replaced the Hollander beater at this time.

By the middle of the nineteenth century, two additional technological developments had taken place that drastically reduced paper permanence and durability. The first of these developments was the use of rosin as a sizing agent. Over time, paper sized with rosin tends to become brittle as the rosin oxidizes. Alum, the acid salt originally introduced as a preservative in gelatin sizing, was also used with rosin sizing.

The second major technological development in nineteenth century papermaking had an even greater adverse affect on paper permanence and durability. By the middle of the nineteenth century, groundwood was already widely used in paper manufacture as the demand for paper exceeded the supply of rags available for its manufacture. Groundwood pulp is made by simply grinding up logs from which the bark has been removed. Papers made from groundwood are not durable because the cellulose fibers in groundwood are very short, and they are not permanent because naturally occurring organic acids, such as lignin and pitch, remain in the pulp and are carried into the finished paper.

Although a significant decline in paper permanence had been noted as early as 1829, when the English clergyman John Murray remarked that a Bible only 13 years old was "crumbling literally into dust" (Barrow 1974), the true cause of this decline was only dimly perceived. During the late nineteenth century, the use of groundwood was generally blamed for the evident decline in paper durability. In 1901, however, Edwin Sutermeister, a paper chemist, realized that "the fault lay not in the basic material but how it was used and what was added to it" (S. D. Warren Company 1981). Permanent papers *can* be made from softwood fibers, if the pulp is first processed to remove the natural plant acids. If these acids are allowed to remain in the groundwood, or if the chlorine bleach is not completely rinsed out of the pulp, or if alum and rosin sizing are used, the paper produced will be impermanent. Many groundwood papers suffer from all three sources of acid.

Brittle paper resulting from acidity caused by papermaking procedures and adverse storage conditions. This book was published in 1940, and the photograph taken about 1970. (Courtesy of the Conservation Division, New York Public Library, Astor, Lenox and Tilden Foundations)

Commercial production of acid-free paper began in the 1950s when fillers and sizing materials compatible with acid-free papers were developed. Modern acid-free papers generally consist of rag fibers or of softwood fibers processed to remove the lignin and other acids. When softwood is used, the fibers are thoroughly rinsed to remove all chlorine bleach, an alkaline sizing is added instead of alum and rosin, and calcium carbonate is mixed with clay fillers to make the paper brighter and more opaque and to act as an acid buffer.

Testing Paper Permanence and Durability

Laboratories evaluate paper permanence and durability by the following parameters: 1) folding endurance, 2) tear resistance, 3) alum, rosin, and groundwood content, 4) metal carbonate content, 5) pH, and 6) fiber analysis, according to length and type.

Since folding endurance in paper tends to degrade more rapidly than any other characteristic, the folding endurance test is considered the most sensitive indicator of a paper's permanence and durability (S. D. Warren Company 1981). According to the above parameters, a permanent/durable paper would have excellent folding endurance and tear resistance; no alum, rosin or groundwood; adequate levels of metal carbonates as an acid buffer; a moderately high pH; and long rag or softwood fibers.

Technically, *acid-free papers* have a pH of 7 or more and no free acids; *alkaline reserve papers* have a pH of 8.5 or greater and contain carbonate buffers to neutralize any acid reaching the paper from the atmosphere or through acid migration from other substances. Acid-free and alkaline reserve papers are becoming more widely available, but they still represent only a very small fraction of the paper market.

Paper labelled and sold as 'acid-free' or 'alkaline-reserve' generally meets these requirements, but paper from each newly purchased package can be tested using a pH testing pen. A dot of ink from the pen will turn yellow on papers with a low pH and blue on papers with a high pH.

Important documents should only be recorded on acid-free or alkaline-reserve papers. Alternatively, original documents may be created on less permanent paper and photocopied on acid-free paper. Many commercial photocopying services now offer the option of acid-free paper for an additional charge.

Extrinsic Enemies of Paper Records

Acid Migration

Acid migration occurs when acid moves from material with a high acid content into material with a lower acid content. Paper records can be damaged by acid migration from newspaper clippings, file folders, wood, some adhesives, cardboard, rubber bands, some inks, and many other acid materials. Even acid-free or alkaline-reserve paper will deteriorate if stored in contact with acidic papers or folders. Important paper records should be kept in acid-free folders and stored in non-oxidizing metal or acid-free cardboard containers. Only photocopies of newspaper clippings should be stored with important paper records. Card files should not be stored in wooden file boxes.

Paper records kept in bound notebooks are particularly prone to damage from acid migrating into the records from the cardboard covers. These covers can be removed prior to storing the notebooks or several sheets of acid-free paper can be inserted in the notebooks as a buffer between the covers and the records.

Light

Light weakens and discolors paper and fades non-permanent ink. Light breaks the cellulose molecules in paper into oxycellulose and hemicellulose, two unstable acid-producing substances, so it adversely affects both paper permanence and paper durability. Invisible ultraviolet (UV) radiation and short wavelength light in the visible blue/violet range of the spectrum are particularly dangerous. Sunlight can consist of as much as 25% UV radiation and fluorescent light can consist of as much as 7%. Although UV light is the most damaging, even visible light will hasten the deterioration of paper and the fading of non-permanent ink. Paper with a high acid content, such as newsprint or any paper made from groundwood, is particularly susceptible to light damage.

Paper records should be protected from light, particularly from sunlight or fluorescent light, whenever possible. Important papers should be kept in closed containers. In the field, paper records should be kept in the shade as much as possible, particularly if they have a high acid content.

Joan Schall taking the blood pressure of Pere Villager Alois Paniu, while colleague Barbara Roll records results, Manus Province, Papua New Guinea, 1982. Often researchers cannot avoid working in areas of strong sunlight. Keeping papers in the shade as much as possible helps mitigate light damage. (Courtesy of F. Roll, Carmel, California)

Heat

Heat accelerates any destructive chemical reaction occurring in paper such as oxidation and acid hydrolysis. The chemical activity of most substances roughly doubles with every 18° F (10° C) increase in temperature. Conversely, the useful life of paper is doubled with every 18° F (10°C) decrease in temperature. Paper deteriorates more slowly in cool storage environments, and the cooler the storage environment, the longer paper will last. Important papers should be stored at the lowest possible temperature at which they can comfortably be used, usually 65–70° F (18–21° C). Paper records should also be protected from temperature fluctuation as much as possible.

In the field, paper records should be protected from high temperatures or dramatic temperature variations by keeping them in the shade whenever possible. Paper records should be stored in cool, stable environments, not in attics, car trunks, or against the outside walls of buildings.

All that is left of one of Charles Darwin's letters from a collection that was stored in plastic envelopes in a Florida attic. The damaged ones were fused together in a group and have been virtually impossible to restore. (Courtesy of the American Philosophical Society Library)

Humidity

Paper is a hygroscopic material (it readily absorbs moisture); consequently, the moisture content of paper generally reflects the ambient relative humidity. Documents become brittle and crack in environments with very low relative humidity (40% or less). In most climates, however, paper records are more likely to suffer damage from high relative humidity.

Documents warp, wrinkle, and become dimensionally unstable when the relative humidity is high, and water-soluble inks run. Like heat, high relative humidity accelerates many of the destructive chemical reactions occurring in paper and hastens its deterioration. Important paper records should be kept in environments with a relative humidity of between 40 and 60% whenever possible.

High humidity also encourages foxing and the growth of mold and mildew on paper surfaces. Foxing appears as red or brown stains on paper made from pulp processed with metal beaters, and occurs when mold reacts with small metallic particles left in the paper.

Paper records should be protected from environments with extremely high, or extremely low, relative humidity as much as possible, and they should also be protected from extreme fluctuations in relative humidity. These fluctuations cause repeated expansion and contraction of the cellulose fibers in paper and adversely affect its structural integrity. Paper records should not be kept in very arid or very humid environments for lengthy intervals.

Anthropologists or archaeologists working in very arid environments where documents tend to become brittle might consider simple expedients for increasing relative humidity in the storage area by placing shallow pans of water near the records. Researchers working in humid tropical areas might consider placing small bags of a dessicant such as silica gel in record storage containers. Silica gel is highly hygroscopic. It changes color as it becomes saturated and can be re-used simply by heating it until the color change is reversed, indicating that the silica gel is dry.

Biological Agents

Microscopic biological agents such as bacteria, actinomycetes,

Laurence Joline measuring the elevation of a Byzantine amphora from a wire grid 120 feet below the surface at Yassi Ada, Turkey, 1961. Some fieldwork takes place under unavoidably humid conditions. (The University Museum, University of Pennsylvania, H. Greer, photographer)

mold and mildew are present in every environment. Under favorable conditions, these microscopic enemies will proliferate, causing cellulose destruction and extensive staining of the document surface, obliterating any information recorded there.

Mold and mildew growth on paper records is a serious problem in humid tropical environments. Paper records should be kept as cool and as dry as possible. Sunlight also discourages mold and mildew growth, but tends to discolor paper and fade ink. Where mold and mildew growth are serious problems, however, it is probably preferable to risk light damage rather than the more serious damage from mold and mildew growth. Paper records should be stored in environments with a relative humidity of 60% or less to prevent mold and mildew growth.

Macroscopic biological agents also attack paper records. Termites, cockroaches, clothes moths, silverfish, bookworms, booklice, and rodents feed on the cellulose in paper and also devour organic adhesives. In field areas sustaining large insect and rodent populations, paper records should be kept in closed metal containers whenever possible. Field records infested with insects should be fumigated *prior* to shipping. Orthopenyl phenol is probably the safest fumigation chemical currently available.

Environmental Pollution

Atmospheric pollutants abound in cities, in industrial areas, and near highways, that is, nearly everywhere paper records are likely to be found. Atmospheric pollutants include gaseous pollutants such as sulphur oxides, nitrogen oxides, and hydrogen sulfide; and particulate matter such as dirt, dust, soot, and mold spores. Cigarette smoke is another common source of environmental pollution.

Gaseous pollutants combine with the natural moisture in paper to produce sulphuric and nitric acids or cause oxidation in cellulose fibers. Dust, soot, and dirt stain documents making them difficult to read, and they tear or grind the cellulose fibers by abrasive action. Particulate pollution, especially soot, is extremely difficult, if not impossible, to remove. These airborne particles also serve as vehicles by which gaseous pollutants such as sulphur dioxide reach the paper surface.

Paper records should be protected from environmental pollution. They should be kept in closed containers to prevent particulate matter from contaminating the surface of the records, and they should only be stored in environments with acceptably low levels of gaseous pollution. They should not be stored in car trunks.

Pencils and Inks

Early manuscript and printing inks consisted of tiny particles of carbon, soot, or lampblack suspended in gum arabic, water, or boiled linseed oil. These inks are time-consuming and relatively expensive to manufacture, but they tend to be harmless to paper,

J. Alden Mason and Burt Bascom pursuing their Tepehuan linguistic studies in Babor-igame, Chihuahua, Mexico, 1951. Carbon typewriter ribbon is one of the most permanent and least harmful of all writing media, along with soft lead pencil. (The University Museum, University of Pennsylvania)

light-fast, and permanent. Modern inks are made from less permanent dyes and may contain additives that reduce the permanence of the written image and of the underlying paper substrate as well. Printers ink is generally not water soluble, but many writing inks will run or smear in very humid conditions. Writing inks should not be used to record field data in tropical environments. The ink in many felt-tip pens is particularly prone to running and fading.

Soft pencil and carbon typewriter ribbons are the most permanent and least harmful writing media. Paper records in pencil can often

35

be photocopied by adjusting the setting on the photocopying machine for light records. Alternatively, field data can be recorded using felt-tip, ballpoint, or fountain pens and photocopied on acid-free paper. Bag labels should generally be written in pencil.

Adhesives

Pressure-sensitive labels and pressure sensitive tapes such as cellophane tape, typewriter correction tape, and masking tape are real foes of paper records. Fastening, mending, labelling, or corrections achieved using pressure-sensitive tapes or labels are extremely short-lived. After several years, the adhesive on pressure-sensitive tapes and labels separates from its paper or cellophane carrier and the carrier falls off. The adhesive, however, remains on the document, permanently staining it and chemically damaging it. Pressure sensitive tapes and labels should never be used on important paper records.

Rubber cement is another harmful adhesive. Like pressure-sensitive tape, the bonding achieved by rubber cement is only temporary, but the sticky residue and staining it causes are permanent. Animal glues bond longer and do less damage, but they can be difficult to remove.

Safer methods for fastening and mending paper records are described below.

Mechanical Damage

Cellulose fibers are broken or ruptured each time paper is folded or flexed, weakening the paper at the site of the fold. Paper records should be bent and folded as little as possible.

Important paper records should be stored flat. If they are stored upright or on edge, they should be supported by an even pressure on both sides and not permitted to sag or crumple. Paper records stored in filing cabinets should not brush against the exterior of the filing cabinet as the drawers slide in and out.

Fasteners

All mechanical fasteners damage paper to some extent. Paper clips made of steel or other metals that rust or corrode will progressively adhere to paper records as they deteriorate until it becomes impossible to remove the clip without removing part of the document. Steel staples also rust and damage paper records.

Rubber bands should never be used on paper records. Rubber bands tear or abrade documents, and they deteriorate over time, losing their elasticity, breaking, and becoming stuck to the paper.

Fasteners should be used on important paper records only when it is essential to do so and the correct arrangement, association, or sequence of the papers cannot otherwise be established. Inert plastic clips or aluminum or stainless steel staples may be used when necessary.

Care of Important Paper Records

Cleaning

Superficial dirt can be removed from paper records using a soft, clean, acid-free cloth, eraser crumbs, a white vinyl or gum eraser, or an archivists' cleaning pad.

Document cleaning with eraser crumbs or an archivists cleaning pad are probably the safest methods for removing surface dirt. The document should be cleaned *gently* from the center outward, without removing any writing or tearing the edges. Eraser crumbs are shaken on the center of the document and gently rubbed over dirty areas. The crumbs are then removed using a soft clean paintbrush. Stubborn stains may be gently removed using a white vinyl or gum eraser.

Mending

Pressure-sensitive tape, rubber cement, or glue should never be used to mend important paper records. The most important axiom in caring for damaged paper records is the rule of reversibility: no treatment should be undertaken that cannot subsequently be reversed.

One of the oldest methods for mending torn paper records is probably still the best. This method uses strips of Japanese tissue paper and rice starch or wheat starch paste. Japanese tissue paper and vegetable starches can be purchased from archival supply houses. Only small quantitites of the paste should be mixed at one time since the paste does not keep well unless preservatives are added. Starch paste is applied to strips of tissue paper with a small soft brush and the strips are placed over the tear. Methyl cellulose paste is another flexible, long-lasting, and reversible adhesive.

British Museum tape is much easier to use. This tape is pH neutral and reversible, but the mend achieved using British Museum tape is not as strong as the mend achieved using Japanese tissue paper and vegetable starch paste.

Some archivists use heat-set mending tape. This tape is placed over a tear and set with a small iron. Heat-set tape is easy to use, but its long-term success and reversibility have not conclusively been established.

Encapsulation

As an alternative to mending, torn or fragmentary paper records can be reconstructed and placed in clear polyester folders. Polyester is an inert, long-lasting plastic. Polyester folders are available from archival supply houses in a wide range of sizes. The folders protect important documents from further insult and hold the pieces of torn documents in place by a slight static charge.

Polyester encapsulation is an excellent method for reconstructing or preserving large paper records, such as site maps or profiles, and for protecting them from further damage resulting from their continued use. Large documents are encapsulated by placing them between sheets of polyester film approximated using double-sided tape. Properly encapsulated documents never touch the tape and are held in place only by the slight static charge of the polyester. Polyester film encapsulation is easy to reverse and completely safe for paper records.

Anthropologists and archaeologists who use large paper documents such as site plans or maps in the field should consider encapsulating them or placing them in polyester sleeves. Polyester sleeves will protect the papers from flogging by wind, trampling, and other sources of mechanical damage, as well as from dirt and smudging.

Photocopying

Field data recorded on irretrievably damaged original documents often can be salvaged by photocopying them on acid-free or alkaline reserve paper. Legible documents deteriorating as a result

Encapsulation table, The University Museum Archives. (The University Museum, University of Pennsylvania)

of acid hydrolysis are particularly good candidates for this method.

Photocopies produced by heat-fusion processes, such as "Xeroxing," are generally stable and permanent. Photocopies produced by photochemical reproduction processes, particularly "wet process" methods, tend to discolor and deteriorate after several years. Copies made using photochemical processes will need to be recopied.

Conservation of Damaged Paper Records

The restoration or cleaning of particularly valuable original documents should only be undertaken by professional paper conservators. Conservation services include paper deacidification, mending, cleaning, reinforcement, and leafcasting. Leafcasting is a process that fills holes or gaps in documents with new paper.

The considerable skill and long hours required for paper conservation are usually reflected in the cost of paper conservation services. If a document is valuable *as an original* then the cost of paper conservation treatments may be well spent. If a document is valuable only for the information it contains, then this information may be less expensively preserved by photocopying it on acid-free paper.

CHAPTER 3. FILM, TAPE, AND VIDEO

Eleanor M. King

Recommendations

Film

- Choose the lowest speed (ASA/ISO number), finest grain film possible for the lighting conditions.

- Document your research with black and white photographs as well as color, because black and white film has greater archival longevity.

- Keep your camera equipment clean and free of dust. In hot climates, avoid leaving it in sunshine or in enclosed spaces such as glove compartments and trunks.

- Store film, photographic paper, and equipment in the field in as cool a place as possible, inside waterproof and dustproof containers. Leave film inside the sealed package until ready to use, and keep it in the camera for as short a time as possible.

- If film is sent out to be processed, choose laboratories that feature archival-quality procedures, including extra washing to remove all destabilizing chemicals.

- Prepare a master set of selected slides and prints to keep in optimum storage, from which a duplicate working set can be made for studying, lecturing, and other routine uses.

- For color storage use a low ASA film processed by a parent lab like Eastman Kodak (*e.g.*, Kodachrome 64). For color projection use Ektachrome, because it withstands heat better. The best black and white film to use for both storage and study is any fine-grained, slow-speed variety.

- Select special encasing products for storage of both master and duplicate sets: acid-free neutral paper for negatives and prints, uncoated polyester or cellulose acetate slide enclosures.

- Cold storage is optimal for all film, but essential for color film. Keep original negatives and master slides and prints in a frost-free refrigerator, or as cool an environment as possible. Relative humidity should be between 30 and 45%.

- Check the master sets and originals regularly for signs of deterioration and regularly replace any damaged items.

- Keep an up-to-date log on the stored masters and originals, detailing basic information on the photograph (subject, date, film) and its condition. Make sure that each negative, slide, and print is appropriately labelled to correspond with the log.

- Use only a soft lead pencil for writing on the backs of prints or on the cardboard mounts of slides.

- Copy motion picture film onto cartridge format for convenient reference.

- Store original motion picture film reels under the same environmental conditions as photographs, but flat to avoid sagging. Keep in acid-free boxes and/or inert plastic bags and avoid taping the leader.

- Make separate master tapes of magnetic motion picture soundtracks, and keep with other magnetic media under appropriate storage conditions.

Sound and Video Recordings

- Use high quality tape for video and sound recordings. If using cassette tapes for sound recording, avoid buying tapes longer than 90 minutes, as they are thin, brittle, and subject to tearing, buckling, and cinching.

- Store originals and make copies for working use. Periodically check alignment of all working tapes, and be sure leader is sufficient to prevent damage in threading on videotapes and reel-to-reels.

- Store tapes vertically on grounded metal shelves or racks, in a dust-free and fireproof environment. Acid-free boxes or inert plastic bags are recommended. A two-foot separation should be maintained between shelves and all electrical fixtures and power lines.

- Temperature and humidity in the tape storage area should not fluctuate, and should avoid extremes of either heat or cold (*i.e.*, do not refrigerate). An average of 62–68° F (17–20° C) and a relative humidity of 30– 40% provide an appropriate climate. Tapes should be kept out of direct sunlight.

- Handle tapes carefully, using lint-free cotton gloves. Clean playback equipment regularly, making sure heads especially are dirt-free and operative.

- Rewind all tapes regularly (once a year) to prevent bleed-through.

Photographs and Research

Photographs have long been an important source of information in anthropological and archaeological studies. Ever since the early days of photography in the 1800s, enterprising researchers have lugged unwieldy equipment into remote areas to record the strange, the exotic, the unknown. Some of the finest collections of early prints, like those of the Bonfils family on the Near East and Mediterranean, or Maler's from Central America, document lifeways that have vanished or ruins now further damaged by time. The past fifty years, however, have seen an ever-increasing use of film as a prime recording medium. Expensive cameras and a healthy film budget are now indispensable parts of most project proposals, and frequently researchers may be observed juggling a couple of different cameras and several different lenses at once.

Most of this increased documentation has been in color. Ever since the early color prints of the 1940s, the color film industry has boomed, with new refinements in technology regularly enhancing the quality of color documentation. Many researchers today in fact document only in color, with black and white being reserved for a few feature shots on some excavations, or for evocative ethnographic stills. This increase is both unavoidable and disturbing from an archival viewpoint. Photographs in general provide clear, accurate records of what the researcher saw, serving as both checks and mnemonic devices for later recall. Color only adds to this capability. In terms of longevity, however, color is a disaster. Unless kept under strictly controlled storage conditions, color will not last more than a few decades. Some films will even start fading and deteriorating in the span of a few

William Henry Jackson photographing Laguna Pueblo, New Mexico, in the 1870s. (Courtesy of the Smithsonian Institution)

years. Black and white films, though more resistant than color, will also fade, if improperly stored, within 40 years—an archivally unacceptable period of time. While nothing can be done to stop the current trend in documentation, this chapter is aimed toward providing researchers with a working knowledge of photographs and their deterioration problems. All film will be covered, but special attention will be given throughout to color. Motion picture reels are included in this discussion. The final section deals with the magnetic media of sound and video recordings, as well as the new videodisk optical technology.

The Photographic Process

Much has been written about photography from a technical and aesthetic point of view. What is important for conservation purposes, however, are the physical changes that produce images from the interaction of film and light in the camera and in the lab. Photography is essentially a chemical process. It depends on the sensitivity to light of silver halides, binary compounds made up of silver and another element, such as iodine or bromine.

Photographic film consists of a silver halide, or usually a combination of halides dispersed in a gelatin medium, which is backed by a plastic support such as cellulose acetate. When light hits the silver halides, they are chemically changed, acquiring a kind of chemical predisposition or sensitivity. Further chemicals added during development act on the latent image contained in the film. The silver halides that were exposed to light are reduced to fine particles of silver metal that look black and reflect the intensity of the light to which they were exposed. The result is an image—the negative—where the lightest areas are dark and the darkest light. The positive, or print, entails further chemical manipulation.

The actual photographic process involves several steps. When light strikes the film in the camera, the silver halides form a latent image, which needs to be protected from further light as the halides are still chemically reactive. In the dark room, a chemical mixture, the developer, is applied, causing the exposed silver halides to convert to blackened particles of silver that clump together to form the visible photographic image. The chemicals in the developer all have specific functions in this process. A solvent, usually water, acts as a medium for the other chemicals. A reducer causes the actual chemical breakdown of the exposed silver halides. Simultaneously, an activator makes the developing solution alkaline rather than acidic, and softens the gelatin emulsion of the film so that the reducer can separate the silver halides. A preservative retards the oxidation of the reducer, thereby preventing rust-colored staining of the film. Finally, a restrainer controls the action of the developing agents so that they do not attack unexposed as well as exposed silver halide grains.

The film is then placed in a stop bath that impedes further action by the developer. Next the film is moved to a fixer or "hypo" solution (so-called because it used to be hyposulphite of soda) that dissolves unexposed silver halide grains, thereby eliminating the film's sensitivity to light. The hypo also contains a hardener to prevent scratching of the emulsion. Finally, water is used to wash off the fixer, because unless negatives are thoroughly rinsed, the remaining hypo will continue to work and bleach out the image. Other products often used during processing include a hypo eliminator, which neutralizes the fixer and reduces the amount of washing needed, and a wetting agent, which reduces the surface tension of the rinse water so that the negative will dry without water marks or streaks.

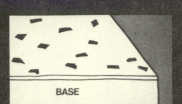

When you take a picture, light reflected from the scene strikes the film and makes a latent image. This image is invisible. It is made visible by processing in special chemicals.

Film is full of tiny light-sensitive silver halide particles. The particles that have been struck by light turn black when they are processed in the first chemical—the developer.

The particles that have not been struck by light will not change in the developer.

The unexposed silver grains are later made soluble by a processing step called fixing and are washed out of the film.

The remaining particles of black metallic silver have formed a visible image, called a negative, in which the original tones are reversed. The light parts of the scene are dark, and the dark parts are light.

Synopsis of the photographic process. (Courtesy of Eastman Kodak Company)

For positives, the whole process is essentially repeated a second time. Printmaking entails shining light through the reversed-image negative onto photographic paper, which, like film, contains light-sensitive silver halides in a gelatin emulsion. The light areas in the negative thus become dark on the paper. The latter is then subjected to the same steps as the original negative: developer, stop bath, fixer, wash.

The point of this description is that a number of chemicals and on-going chemical reactions are involved at every stage of the photographic process. No matter how much care is taken in development, the final product, whether negative, slide, print, or motion picture film, will contain chemical residues that will continue to react chemically long after the document has left the lab.

The problem of preservation is compounded for color films, which essentially work the same way as black and whites. The color comes from dyes that are suspended with the silver halides in three layers of gelatin emulsion, each layer of a different color sensitivity. Like the emulsion, the dyes are organic. Processing is more complicated for these films. It involves the same kind of procedures as black-and-white development, but multiplied, as numerous baths are needed to define the color. Chemicals are used to bring out the image, fix it, and wash away excess dye and halides. Again, chemical reactions do not stop once the film is processed. In addition, the organic dyes decompose over time. They can change a great deal in just a few years. Color films are thus less stable than black and whites.

Causes of Film Deterioration

The chemical stability of photographic records is affected by a number of factors. We have already noted that chemical residues left over from processing can cause problems if chemical reactions continue. Over time, photographs, negatives, and motion picture film can fade or become spotted. Similarly, if the processing is incomplete for whatever reason, deterioration can occur. For example, if the hypo fails to wash out all the unexposed silver halides, the product may remain sensitive to light. The instability of color dyes has also been mentioned.

Equally problematic are the materials that make up the film itself or that support prints. Modern photographic film is usually composed of at least five layers, as follows: a top coat of hard gelatin that protects the emulsion from scratching; the emulsion itself, which consists, as noted, of silver halide particles suspended in a gelatin medium; a subbing, or glue-like substance, which holds the emulsion layer to the base; a support material, usually a plastic such as cellulose acetate or polyester; and finally an anti-curl/anti-halation backing, which prevents light from reflecting off the support layer or the back of the camera during exposure, thus creating halos or blurriness in the image. All these materials can have problems of stability. Gelatin and subbings can decompose. Supports also can be problematic, as witnessed by the high flammability and rapid deterioration characteristic of films on a nitrocellulose base.

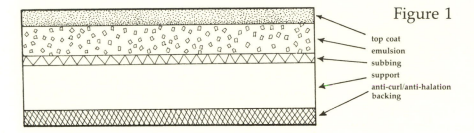

Figure 1

top coat
emulsion
subbing
support
anti-curl/anti-halation backing

Diagram of the layers in photographic film. (Drawing by Georgianna Grentzenberg, The University Museum, University of Pennsylvania)

Print support materials—usually paper—can also be short- lived. Resin-coated (RC) paper, for instance, is often used for publicity shots because of its high glossy quality and ability to be quickly processed, yet the pigmented polyethylene with which it is coated degrades rapidly in the presence of light and/or changing humidity. In addition, its multi-layer composition inhibits washing, as the layers become unstuck. Residual chemicals thus remain on the surface and can also seep under the layers into the paper itself. Finally, the organic substances in film, especially color film, are subject to the same kind of attack by biological agents as paper. Mold, mildew, bacteria, insects, and rodents eat away at photographic materials, the danger they present increasing with high humidity.

All these factors need not be severe problems in and of themselves. They are in effect preconditions to future problems, as perhaps the most important circumstances affecting film and print stability are the conditions of storage. Proper storage can do much to mitigate the damage incurred during processing or the inevitable deterioration of component materials. Atmospheric conditions have an especially significant impact on photographic records. Light and high heat and humidity all affect negatives, slides, prints, and motion picture film adversely. Also noxious are atmospheric contaminants such as dust and oxidizing gases. Hydrogen sulfide and sulfur dioxide, for instance, cause gradual sulfiding of the silver image, seen as an overall yellow stain on prints and film, as well as slow deterioration of gelatin. Contaminants and excessive light, heat, and/or humidity interact with chemical residues and unstable component materials to accelerate the process of decomposition.

Other storage conditions that affect photographic stability are the physical materials that surround the documents. Mounting boards, mounting tissue, inks, adhesives, adhesive tapes, paper, and plastic sheeting can all affect the silver image or its support in long-term storage. Acid materials deteriorate chemically (see Chapter 2). Some inks are acid and eat their substrate. Adhesives lose tackiness and can stain or damage documents. Unstable plastics react with residual chemicals in photographs. Choice of archivally sound encasement materials can alleviate many problems of deterioration.

Film Types and Temporal Stability

Another major set of factors affecting the permanence of photographic records is subsumed by the type of film used, as films vary in their susceptibility to deterioration. The two characteristics that most affect preservation for black and white films are speed and grain size. Speed can be defined as the sensitivity of the film to light. It is usually described by an ASA (American Standards Association) or ISO (International Standards Organization) number. The higher the speed, and therefore the ASA or ISO, the more sensitive the film is to light. This sensitivity is obviously an advantage for low-light photography. It can also be a problem, however, as it means that the film is very quick to react to any light stimulus. High-speed films require particularly thorough immersion in the hypo solution to eliminate completely non-exposed silver halides. Grain size in film refers to the bunching of the reduced silver (metallic silver) in the emulsion of the negative. It is related to speed, in that the higher the film ASA, the larger the grain. Large grain size, like high ASA, means that subsequent reactions and breakdown will occur faster.

Films should be chosen with these characteristics in mind, which manufacturers conveniently list on film boxes. Though certain situations might require high-speed, large-grained films, frequently an acceptable result can be obtained by using a lower-speed, finer-grained film. Plus-X-Pan, for example, is a black and white film often mentioned by the researchers interviewed in our survey. With an ASA of 125, it is of medium speed and has a moderately fine grain. For most routine research photography, it is clearly preferable to Tri-X-Pan, which, with an ASA of 400, has a higher speed and a grain that is not as fine.

Color film offers its own set of characteristics and problems. As noted above, it is inherently more unstable than black and white, with shifts in color and density occurring over time. Color is particularly subject to fading and/or staining in the light, but similar results can occur even in dark storage, if heat and humidity are not properly controlled. High-speed color films are thus even more at risk than comparable speed black and whites. A considerable amount of work has been done on the relative stability of different kinds of color film (see Wilhelm 1979). An easy, general index to follow is that dye combinations that emphasize the "warmer" or red end of the color spectrum, such as Kodachrome, seem to last longer in storage (whether exhibited or in the dark) than those that highlight the "cooler" or blue end of the spectrum, like Ektachrome. On the other hand, Ektachrome is more resistant to the intense, brief heat of a slide projector, and is therefore the best film for frequent classroom or lecture use.

The reason for differences in color stability lies in the type of processing the film requires. The most common is the chromogenic process, which entails first the development of silver halides with a developer, then a conversion of dye couplers to color dyes in the presence of an oxidized developer. Films like Kodacolor, Vericolor II and Ektachrome, which have dye couplers incorporated directly into their emulsions, are not as stable as films such as Kodachrome, for which the couplers are introduced during the processing. For the former, unused dye couplers remain in the negative or print after processing, thereby creating an unstable chemical environment. Also destabilizing in Ektachrome are residual chemicals left behind in the very short washing times necessitated by its processing. The most stable print process now widely available is Cibachrome, a silver-dye-bleach process in which preformed dyes in the emulsion are selectively removed (see Wilhelm 1979). The least stable are the instant print processes yielding unique photographs with no negatives or transparencies to make additional copies. If instant prints are important to the documentary record, they should be copied onto more stable film.

The instability of color film is a critical factor to weigh in choosing how to document a project photographically. Researchers might consider shifting their emphasis from color to black and white, or at least documenting in black and white as well as color so they have overlapping coverage. Black and white retains its image longer than color. Once the color changes and the image fades, nothing remains to record the research.

Alfred Bendiner's rendition of how contemporary archaeologists document discoveries, in this case Stela X at the site of Tikal, Guatemala. Whether there are several photographers or only one, using different cameras for black and white and for color film is one way of ensuring overlapping coverage. (The University Museum, University of Pennsylvania)

Preservation of Photographic Records

The first domain in which to ensure permanence is processing. There are advantages and disadvantages to going to commercial laboratories or developing images oneself. For black and whites, the choice is frequently made on a financial basis, as it is cheaper for researchers to do their own processing. Color film, on the other hand, is usually given to a commercial lab, because few researchers know how to process it. If a commercial outfit is chosen, the researcher can insist on certain procedures to minimize the risk of residual chemicals. Stop baths and print-fixing baths can be tested to see if they are fresh or exhausted. Other tests exist for residual silver or hypo. Prints and negatives can be washed longer so that all fixatives are securely removed. A hypo eliminator can be used. Finally, protective treatments such as Kodak GP–1 have been developed that render the silver image more resistant to later attack by atmospheric contaminants. These same procedures can of course be more rigorously followed if the researcher himself does the developing. For color, it is best to keep in mind the considerations on processing outlined in the section above and choose a process that is both affordable and stable.

Even more critical are storage conditions. It is of paramount importance to control light, air purity, and dust (see Chapter 5). The best kind of storage for negatives, slides, and prints is cold, dark storage, a point demonstrated by Henry Wilhelm (see Bibliography) in a number of accelerated aging tests. He recommends frost-free refrigerators as providing the ideal environment. Kodachrome is said to last up to 100 years if stored under such conditions, and Ektachrome up to 50 years, where in hotter, more humid and lighter conditions the latter can deteriorate significantly within 10.

While cold, dry storage is optimal, there are many situations in which it is not possible. Researchers working in the tropics, for instance, often do not have access to any refrigerated space. The best recourse is to keep film and paper in waterproof and dustproof containers, storing them in as cool a place as possible, and to avoid leaving camera equipment or accessories either in hot sunshine for longer than necessary or in an enclosed space such as a car glove compartment or trunk. Researchers should leave

Danny Walthall taking pictures of architectural features at the site of Las Fosas, Arizona, from the photo tower. In dry environments, special care must be exercised to keep both equipment and film dust-free by constant cleaning, both before and after use. (Courtesy of the Arizona State Museum, The University of Arizona; E. Sires, Photographer)

film in its sealed package until ready to use, and keep it in the camera for as short a time as possible. Exposed film should be processed as soon as possible, and in general only the film and paper necessary should be kept in stock. To avoid moisture condensation on film and lenses if they are kept in air conditioning, they should be allowed to warm up before use.

In hot, dry environments, both equipment and film should be carefully protected from dust and constantly cleaned, before and after use. In humid environments, equipment and film should be checked for fungus. Equipment may be dried out by rigging a small box or cabinet with an electric light bulb or small electric heater element. Film and photographic papers cannot be kept in such enclosures, as the heat will adversely affect them. If their original packaging is not airtight, a desiccant such as silica gel can be enclosed in their waterproof container to protect them from the humidity. Silica gel can also be used to help dehumidify a refrigerator. It can be obtained with a useful indicator dye that changes from deep blue to pink when the substance is saturated. The silica gel can then be dried for a few hours in a hot oven and used again when it regains its blue color. If photographic materials are processed in the tropics, particular care should be taken to remove all residual chemicals to ensure better stability. Finally, film and paper should be kept as far away from contaminants such as paints and lacquers as possible, as the fumes from these products will damage photographic materials (for further information, see Eastman Kodak C–24, 1978).

Slides, negatives, and prints should be stored in archivally sound enclosure materials. The best materials to use for slides are uncoated polyester or cellulose acetate sleeves. Unsafe materials include glassine envelopes and chlorinated, nitrated, or highly plasticized sheeting, which cause deterioration and ferrotyping or staining of the photographic image. There are some simple non-chemical tests to use for safety. The more a plastic smells, the less likely it is to be good for archival or long-term storage. Chemical stability is the clue here, as a product that has a strong odor

Inert plastic enclosures hanging in vertical storage help prolong the longevity of black and white and color slides. (The University Museum, University of Pennsylvania)

is giving off fumes. Also to be avoided are excessively shiny materials. Smooth, glossy surfaces in contact with film can cause it to stick and produce the equivalent of ferrotyping. Finally, pressure on negatives and slides should be minimized. Sheeting should not be too tight, and sheets should not be pressed together or stored flat. Vertical storage and filing is preferred for all photographic materials. Slides should be protected by acetate sleeves and hung in stable plastic enclosures in a file cabinet, or placed in special slide boxes. The latter should be either baked enamel, treated wood, or a plastic lacking chlorine compounds and hydrochloric acid plasticizers. Again, researchers would do best to follow their noses in determining plastic safety. Another criterion to judge by is firmness. Rigid plastic file boxes are by definition not over-plasticized (for more information see Balsley and Moore 1980).

Negatives should be stored in acid-free paper envelopes and filed vertically, preferably in a file cabinet or boxes comparable to those used for slides. Contacts between negatives or between negatives and surfaces other than the acid-free paper should be avoided to prevent ferrotyping.

Valued prints should not be mounted, but rather stored vertically in acid-free folders and boxes, if 8 x 10 inches or smaller. Larger prints should be stored flat to avoid buckling and sagging. Separate prints should be protected by an interleaving sheet of uncoated polyester or cellulose acetate. Working prints, used by researchers, can be mounted on acid-free mounting board with Mylar corners or heat- set tape, as other adhesives are more prone to decompose or react with atmospheric moisture to release damaging compounds. Mounted prints should be stored in the same way as unmounted ones. If a print is to be exhibited, it should be mounted using an acid-free mounting board and mat, rice paper, and wheat starch paste as adhesive (no glue). It should be protected by glass and displayed away from sources of ultraviolet light, especially sunlight. Exhibition time should be limited to no more than three months.

Finally, motion picture reels should be copied onto cartridge format for convenient reference. The reels themselves should be stored flat to avoid problems of sagging and buckling. Cold storage is preferred, as with other photographic documents. The beginning of the film, or leader, should not be taped to the movie reel, as adhesives can damage film. In addition, some motion

The camera and sound crew of the Matto Grosso Expedition filming in Brazil, 1931 (1. to r.: G. Rawls, F. Crosby, Carol, A. Davis, and A. Rossi). Ethnographic movie reels such as those brought back by Vincent M. Petrullo, The University Museum's representative on the Expedition, are valuable sources of information requiring special procedures for preservation. (The University Museum, University of Pennsylvania)

picture films (*e.g.*, Super 8) have magnetic soundtracks that are subject to deterioration (see below). The soundtrack should be copied onto a separate master tape to safeguard against possible loss, and stored separately.

For long-term storage and use of photographic materials, it is best to consider making master and working sets. Prints are easily reproduced, so the greatest care should be taken of negatives. Slides that are frequently used should be duplicated. The master set should be stored under the optimum conditions available, like the negatives, and both types of document checked periodically for signs of deterioration. New copies should be made when any damage begins to show. For slides it would be best to use a low speed, stable-process film to create the master set, and a film such as Ektachrome for the lecture set. Sometimes in the field only local processing is available, so choice of film is restricted to those that can be developed outside specialized labs, like Ektachrome. In those cases, researchers should select the most important shots immediately upon their return, and have copies of those slides or negatives made onto more stable film.

Researchers should keep an up-to-date log on all stored masters and originals. The information recorded should include subject, date, film type, and physical condition of the slide, print, or negative. Each item should be labelled so it corresponds with the log. A soft lead pencil is most appropriate for writing on the backs of prints, the cardboard mounts of slides, or negative enclosures.

Sound Recordings, Video-Tape, and New Optical Technology

Sound recordings and videotapes are both all-electronic media that rely on the use of magnetic tapes similar to those discussed in Chapter 4. They share with film the same intolerance for extreme heat and fluctuations in temperature and humidity. Unlike photographs, magnetic tapes are also sensitive to extreme cold, which can trigger deterioration in videotapes especially (Swartzburg 1980). In addition, magnetic tapes are subject to "cold flow," or unequal stresses and strains wound into the tape as it is being played. While the strains tend to equalize themselves when a tape is stored, they can be triggered by atmospheric fluctuations (Swartzburg and Boyle 1983).

Working copies should be made for all tapes and the originals stored according to the recommendations outlined for magnetic tape in Chapter 4. Ideal temperature ranges from 62–68° F (17–20° C) and relative humidity from 30–40%. Of particular importance are a dust-free environment and avoidance of electromagnetic fields such as those found in color televisions or microwave ovens. Grounded metal shelves and acid-free containers or inert plastic bags are recommended to minimize the risk of exposure. Electrical outlets and power lines should be no less than two feet away (Swartzburg 1980). Tapes should be kept out of direct sunlight and rewound about once a year to avoid bleed-through, or the mixing of recorded sounds between two separate sections of tape when they lie superimposed. Cotton gloves, as lint-free as possible, should be used when handling stored tapes. Finally, equipment heads should be cleaned regularly if tapes are to be played. Tapes are especially flammable, so fire protection is important in storage areas (see Chapter 5) (Swartzburg and Boyle 1983).

Margaret Mead interviewing Ipak, daughter of Francis Paliau, who holds the tape recorder, Pere Village, Manus Province, Papua New Guinea, 1971. (Courtesy of B. H. Roll, Carmel, California)

While reel-to-reel tapes still provide the best sound fidelity available, cassettes are recommended for most fieldwork, as they are self-contained units, resistant to mishandling, light-weight and simple to use. Cassettes, however, are all designed to occupy a standard amount of space. There is a danger, therefore, with tapes longer than 90 minutes, because they are made thinner to fit into the same box unit. Thin tapes are prone to buckling, tearing and cinching, and should be avoided. Videotape cassettes are likewise preferred over any remaining open-reel, helical-scan formats. Tapes of all kinds should be checked regularly for proper alignment, as misalignment on the spools can cause straining, tearing and other severe damage. The beginning part of the tape, or leader, should be long enough on videotapes and reel-to-reels to prevent damage in threading.

Recently, there has been a great surge of interest in new optical technology and, specifically, videodisks. Each disk, no larger than a standard long-playing record, "is capable of holding a discrete and reproducible image in the form of codes, in either digital (binary) or analog form" (Nghiep Cong Bui 1984:420). These codes are etched into the disk by laser, and consist of a series of "microscopic pits and gouges of varying lengths and spacings arranged in a continuous spiral, much like the grooves of a phonograph record" (*ibid.*). When replayed by refracting a laser beam across the coding, the disk yields textual or pictorial images. As each disk can store up to 108,000 images, videodisk technology is potentially an extremely powerful recording tool. In addition, videodisks, when linked to the appropriate computer program, can be randomly accessed, a recovery method more efficient than the sequential access of microfilm and magnetic tape.

Currently, the technology is still in the experimental stage and very costly, if the initial investment for equipment as well as the disks themselves are considered. Pilot studies, notably in Canada at the Public Archives and National Library, have shown the value of videodisks for storage and retrieval of information. There is as yet little known about durability and permanence, however, although the Library of Congress is in the process of assessing the use of videodisks for preserving endangered paper and other items. The coding of each videodisk is well protected by several plasticized coats, and the disk has the advantage of never being in contact with the read-head mechanism, so there is no wear and tear from friction. No accelerated aging tests have been conducted, however, and the disks are known to be susceptible to chemical corrosion from the environment. Also, each 2.5 mm disk really consists of several layers that are separated by air. It is possible therefore for some internal oxidation and degradation to occur. At present it is too early to say whether solutions to these problems will be found, and what the long- term storage capabilities of videodisks will prove to be.

CHAPTER 4. MACHINE-READABLE RECORDS

Trudy Van Houten

Recommendations

- Machine-readable records created using obsolete or obsolescent hardware and software should be converted to a format compatible with current technology as soon as possible.

- Machine-readable records stored on punchcards should be transferred to magnetic tape or printout immediately. Records stored on tape cassettes, magnetic drums, or magnetic disks should also be transferred to magnetic tape for long- term storage.

- Magnetic tape should be stored at 62–68° F (17–20° C) and between 30–40% relative humidity. Floppy and flexible disks should be stored at 50–125° F (10–52° C) and at 40–70% relative humidity. Fluctuations in temperature and humidity are more damaging than a constant temperature or humidity slightly above or slightly below the optimum range. Prior to use, machine-readable records should be allowed time to acclimate to the environmental conditions of the room in which they will be used.

- Magnetic tape shoud be stored upright on metal racks which support the reel at the hub. Tape reels should be rotated one-quarter turn every three months, and tapes and reels should be checked annually for damage. Floppy and flexible disks should be stored upright with an even lateral pressure, preferably in metal containers.

- Magnetic tapes should be recopied every five to ten years, and replaced every ten to twenty years; floppy and flexible disks should be recopied every two to three years.

- Magnetic storage media should be protected from surface contamination. They should be used only in clean, dust-free environments, and crumbs, fur, dirt, smoke, fingers, vapors from volatile liquids, and other contaminants should never touch the recording surface.

- Machine-readable records should never be exposed to the magnetic fields found in telephones, televisions, some electrical equipment, computer monitor screens, and the tops of diskdrives. Metal storage containers help prevent accidental loss due to interference from foreign magnetic fields.

- At least one backup copy of each important machine-readable file should be maintained and preferably stored in a location different from that in which the original is stored.

- All important machine-readable files should be write-protected unless they are being updated. Master files should only be updated after an identical backup copy of the file has been created.

- Containers for magnetic storage media should carry labels that completely and accurately describe their contents.

- Adequate documentation for each machine-readable record should be prepared and kept current. Minimal documentation includes technical specifications, a codebook, a record layout, and any background information necessary for accessing, using, and understanding the contents of the file.

- Important machine-readable records should be kept in fireproof containers or stored at computer installations with adequate fire safety precautions.

Introduction

Ten years ago, machine-readable records generally consisted of files created in one of several programming languages on large mainframe computers, and these records were generally stored on punchcards, or on magnetic tape, drums, or disks. Recently, however, two phenomena have greatly complicated the relatively simple picture of a decade ago.

The first phenomenon is the extraordinary recent increase in computer hardware, software, and automated storage technology. Instead of just a few mainframe computer models, manufactured

In recent years mini- and microcomputers have invaded most offices and laboratories. Machine-readable data presents special problems of access, retrieval and storage. (Courtesy of the Ban Chiang Project, The University Museum, University of Pennsylvania)

by a handful of industrial giants, the current market now includes hundreds of minicomputers and microcomputers manufactured by fifty or more different companies.

The dramatic proliferation of computer hardware has been surpassed by an even more dramatic proliferation in computer systems and applications software. The number of programming languages has increased steadily over the last decade, but the number of proprietary software packages, designed for use on minicomputers and microcomputers, has increased even more rapidly. Currently available proprietary software packages for smaller computers include generalized word processing, calculation, and database management programs, as well as software packages designed for very specific tasks. For example, an excellent set of programs written in BASIC and designed to facilitate faunal analysis has recently been published (Klein and Cruz-Uribe 1984).

The technology available for storing machine-readable records has also proliferated. Punchcards have now become largely obsolete, but the range of available magnetic storage media is wider than ever, including floppy disks in several sizes and the newer flexible disks. More recently, digitized optical disks have been developed that can store computer-generated maps, plots, and graphs, as well as text and data (see Chapter 3).

The second phenomenon complicating the relatively simple earlier picture of machine-readable records is the determined and extensive penetration of this vast technology into the workplace and home. Paper records now account for less than half of the records generated by the federal government (Ambacher 1985). The development of relatively inexpensive "user-friendly" microcomputers within the last five years has accelerated this trend, and it is likely that machine-readable records will become the dominant form of record-keeping in the near future for most fields.

A considerable amount of anthropological and archaeological research is currently generated, stored, analyzed, and edited on both mainframe and personal computers. More recently, even smaller portable computers have been used to process archaeological, ethnographic, and primatological data in remote field study areas. The rapid transition from paper to machine-readable documentation in the last decade calls for a careful evaluation of the advantages and disadvantages of machine-readable records. This chapter begins with such an assessment and ends with a discussion of short-term and long-term storage considerations for machine-readable records.

Advantages of Machine-Readable Records

The benefits of the recent technological revolution for anthropological and archaeological research are numerous and substantial. Machine-readable records can store vast amounts of data in a small physical space. Approximately 120 books 500 pages in length can be stored on a single standard nine-track computer tape, and approximately 5,000 books can be stored on computer tapes occupying only one cubic foot of space (Ambacher, personal communication 1985).

Machine-readable records can be manipulated easily and rapidly. Automated information can be entered, retrieved, revised, updated, sorted, searched, reformatted, aggregated, summarized, analyzed, and indexed far more quickly than information on cards or paper.

Storing data in machine-readable form also facilitates the exchange of information. Several separate data files can be merged or linked with other files to provide larger statistical samples or more extensive bases for comparison. Automated records can be copied far more rapidly and inexpensively than the comparable volume of data on paper, and telecommunicated to remote locations within hours. At the same time, storing data in machine-readable form also affords greater security since access to sensitive information can be restricted through the use of passwords or by the creation of user copies of databases in which personally identifying characteristics are stripped from the file or disguised.

Co-director Pisit Charoenwongsa and John Hastings study computer reports for the Ban Chiang Project, 1982. Machine-readable records permit the storage and manipulation of larger amounts of data than any other medium. (The University Museum, University of Pennsylvania; D. Gladstone, Photographer)

Disadvantages of Machine-Readable Records

It is ironic that one of the great advantages of machine-readable records, the ease with which they can be revised or reformatted, also entails one of the great disadvantages of machine-readable records, the ease with which they can be unintentionally over-written, partially erased, or completely obliterated. In general, although machine-readable records are easier to create, revise, and reproduce than paper records, they are also far easier to destroy or render useless. Without careful treatment and the requisite hardware, software, and documentation, machine-readable records are only mute pieces of paper or plastic. And, they are fragile and impermanent pieces of paper or plastic at best.

The storage media for machine-readable records are far less permanent than paper and microforms. The polyester magnetic tape used to record machine readable data lasts only 10 to 20 years even under ideal storage and maintenance conditions. The newer floppy disks and flexible disks may last somewhat longer, as their manufacturers claim, but this is by no means certain. Under less than ideal conditions, the deterioration of magnetic storage media is even more rapid.

The pattern of magnetic signals recorded on the tape surface is even less enduring than the tape itself. Hedstrom (1984:27) has described the process by which automated information is stored:

> Recording on magnetic storage media is accomplished by selectively magnetizing the oxide coating of the recording surface in such a way that the presence or absence of a magnetized spot in a given location corresponds to one bit in a binary code. Magnetic media are reusable because the surface can be magnetized and demagnetized many times.

These magnetic patterns can also be drastically rearranged by contact with *any* magnetic field. Magnetic fields strong enough to damage these patterns are found in telephones, magnetic paper clip holders, some power switches and cables, alternators, transformers, televisions, radar signals, airport metal detectors, and even in computer monitor screens and the tops of disk drives. "Print-through," the leakage of signals from one section of magnetic tape to an adjacent section of tape stored on the same reel, can also occur.

The fragile patterns of magnetic signals can also be distorted or destroyed by stretching or creasing of improperly wound tape, by bending floppy disks or flexible disks, and through contamination of the media surface by particles as small as 0.0046 inches in diameter. Common surface contaminants include dust, lint, eraser crumbs, food crumbs, fur, ashes, fingerprints, smoke, and vapors from solvents or other volatile liquids. The likelihood of surface contamination is enhanced by the fact that friction between the recording surfaces of magnetic storage media and the guide surfaces of the tape or disk drive creates a small electrostatic charge that actually attracts surface contaminants.

The optimum environmental range for magnetic storage media is also far narrower than the optimum range for storing paper or microforms, and magnetic storage media are extremely sensitive to rapid changes in temperature or humidity. Fluctuations in temperature and humidity can be even more damaging to magnetic tape than storage at a constant temperature and humidity slightly above, or slightly below, the optimum range. It has been estimated that a five degree change in temperature or a five percent change in relative humidity can cause a magnetic tape 2400 feet long to expand or contract one foot, causing the tape surfaces to slide over one another on the reel with an obvious potential for damage.

The optimum environmental range for floppy disks and flexible disks is somewhat broader, but the newer media should also be protected from temperature and humidity extremes and from rapid temperature change.

It should be emphasized that even machine-readable records stored under ideal conditions can perish from neglect in only ten years. Routine maintenance—including tape cleaning, rewinding, and recopying—is required to prevent the deterioration of magnetic tapes and the loss of the information contained on them. Too often, magnetic tapes do not receive the required care. The State Historical Society of Wisconsin, Archives Division, recently conducted a study of state archives that revealed that in many instances the machine-readable records accessioned by these archives could not be expected to survive even for the relatively brief mandatory retention period, much less for the future (David, Ham, *et al.* 1981). While paper records can usually be safely placed in inactive storage for 50 to 100 years, machine-readable records can survive in inactive storage for only one-tenth of that time.

David Stephen using a programmable calculator to record the provenience and object code for artifacts found at the site of Rooney Ranch, Arizona, 1983. The increasing use of computers in the field heightens the likelihood of surface contamination and the need for routine maintenance. (Courtesy of Pima Community College)

Even if magnetic storage media are protected from physical deterioration through storage under optimum conditions and careful maintenance, their survival as usable information is by no means certain. Hardware and software dependent records may become unusable as the generating hardware or software becomes obsolete and is replaced by incompatible hardware or software. Machine-readable records are *hardware dependent* if they can only be used with a specific type of hardware such as a particular type, brand, or model of computer or plotter; machine-readable records are *software dependent* if they can only be used with a particular type, version, or release of systems or applications software.

In the short term, hardware and software dependence may limit the usefulness of a machine-readable record since it can only be used with a particular machine using a particular program. In the long term, hardware and software dependence may destroy the usefulness of a machine-readable record altogether as the hardware, replacement parts, and software on which it depends become unavailable. The current rapid rate of technological change makes this problem especially acute.

Short-term Storage

Punchcards, Magnetic Disks, Magnetic Drums

Punchcards are currently on the brink of hardware obsolescence if not extinction, because the cardreaders necessary for their input are rapidly disappearing. Punchcards are also prone to tear, and they are generally manufactured from fairly acidic paper. Important machine-readable records stored on punchcards should be transferred to magnetic tape or printout as soon as possible.

The cost of transferring data from punchcards to tapes varies according to the size of the data file but will generally not exceed $50 to $100. Hardcopies can be obtained even less expensively. They should be printed on acid-free paper or later photocopied on acid-free paper.

Magnetic drums and disks are also becoming less common. Data stored on these media should be transferred to magnetic tape or printout. Records stored on tape cassettes should also be transferred to magnetic tape or printout for similar reasons.

Portrait of an endangered species. (Courtesy of the Ban Chiang Project, The University Museum, University of Pennsylvania)

Magnetic Tape

Magnetic tapes are often stored at the computer installations where they are used, for convenience and because the ideal environment for magnetic tapes is also the ideal environment for computers. Off-site storage conditions should approximate this environment as closely as possible. Magnetic tapes should be stored at a constant temperature of 62–68° F (17–20°C) and at a constant relative humidity of 40%. If magnetic tapes are not stored at the computer installation, they should be kept at a temperature and humidity equivalent to that of the computer room in which they will be accessed for 24 hours prior to their use.

Magnetic tapes should be stored upright on metal racks which support the reel at the hub. The tape reel should be rotated one quarter turn every three months, like champagne, to avoid distortion of the tape or reel. Recently, plastic strips have been developed that support the reel uniformly by hanging it. Magnetic tapes should be checked annually for uneven tape winding, creasing, or damage to the reel, hub, or canister, and cleaned and rewound annually or biannually. Tapes should be recopied at least every five or ten years and replaced every ten or twenty years, depending on storage conditions.

Backup copies of all important records should be created; important files should not be changed until the backup copy has been created. All magnetic tape containers should be completely and accurately labelled, and file documentation should be maintained and kept up to date.

Magnetic tapes cannot be overwritten unless a plastic write ring has been inserted in the hub. Canisters containing master copies of important records should bear labels stating "READ ONLY" or "DO NOT USE WRITE RING."

Floppy and Flexible Disks

Floppy disks consist of a polyester recording surface somewhat thicker than magnetic tape. The recording surface is enclosed in a soft plastic sleeve but remains exposed at the hub and through an oval aperture where it is read by the disk drive.

Flexible disks are smaller than floppy disks and their media surface is completely protected by a rigid plastic case, and by a metal

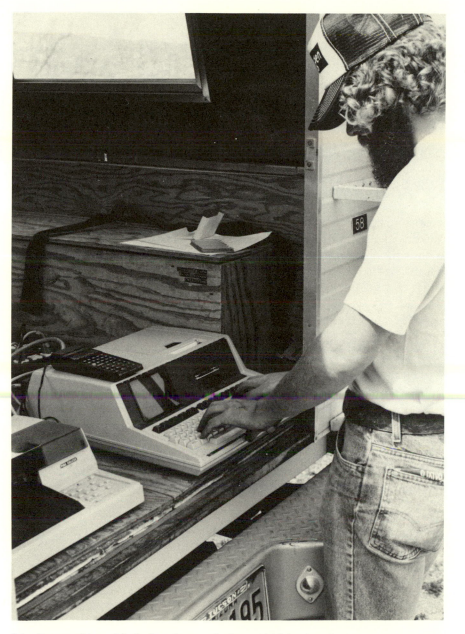

John Rose working with the data from a calculator which has been hooked up to a computer and plotter at the site of Rooney Ranch, Arizona, 1983. Machine-readable records of important field data should be labelled properly and copied to prevent accidental loss of information. (Courtesy of Pima Community College)

shutter which covers the recording surface when the flexible disk is not in use.

The media surface of floppy and flexible disks is better protected than the surface of magnetic tape, and the patterns of recorded magnetic signals on these disks cannot be damaged by improper winding or "print-through." These patterns can be destroyed, however, by bending the disks or by placing heavy objects on them.

Floppy and flexible disks should be stored upright with an even lateral pressure, preferably in metal containers to protect them from magnetic fields. Very important files should be kept in fire-proof containers.

Floppy and flexible disks should be stored at temperatures between 50 and 125° F (10–52° C) and between 40 and 70% relative humidity. Like magnetic tapes, floppy disks and flexible disks require time to acclimate to the environment of the room in which they will be used. If they are stored in a separate location, they should remain in the computer room for several hours prior to use.

All important files should be write-protected. Floppy disks are write-protected by placing a metallic tape over a small notch on the side of the disk sleeve. Flexible disks are write-protected by sliding a small plastic tab within a channel on the back of the disk. Neither of these methods is very satisfactory. The tape tends to fall off the floppy disks and leaves a sticky residue on the disk sleeve when it is removed. The tabs on the flexible disks tend to slip out of position or to fall out of the channel altogether. It is important to confirm that these devices are in place each time the disk is used. Write-protected disks should carry labels bearing this reminder.

Many of the manufacturers of floppy and flexible disks consulted in compiling this report claimed virtually unlimited longevity for machine-readable records stored on these disks. There are several reasons to be skeptical about these claims. Like magnetic tapes, the media surfaces of floppy and flexible disks consist of an unstable polyester that tends to deteriorate even under optimum environmental conditions, and the magnetic signals recorded on these disks are likely to fade. Important files should be recopied every few years, regardless of manufacturers' claims.

Floppy disks and flexible disks are also at risk from hardware and software obsolescence. It is important to make sure that these disks will be compatible with current technology when the time comes to convert them to long-term storage.

Backup copies of all important files should be created, and master files should not be updated unless an identical backup copy exists. Adequate documentation should be maintained and kept up to date for all important files. A sample documentation form appears in Figure 2.

Long-term Storage

Guidelines for the long-term storage of machine-readable records are more difficult to formulate. At present, *no* magnetic storage medium meets archival standards for permanence and durability. While several promising long-term storage media are currently under study, scholars and archivists cannot afford to wait until the newer technologies have been developed, tested, and distributed. The following guidelines represent a consensus of current opinion on the long-term preservation of machine-readable records. These guidelines are offered only as interim solutions, however, until better storage technologies can be developed.

At present, magnetic tape is the standard long-term storage medium for machine-readable records. Although magnetic tape is not an archival storage medium, its shortcomings are at least fairly well understood. Until more satisfactory media for long-term storage are developed, most archivists concerned with storing machine-readable records agree that they should be stored on high-quality certified nine-track 1/2 inch tape recorded at 1600 bytes per inch. Records stored on punchcards or magnetic drums and magnetic disks should be recopied onto magnetic tape. Records stored on tape cassettes, floppy disks, and flexible disks should be telecommunicated to a mainframe computer and recorded on magnetic tape.

Magnetic tapes intended for long-term preservation should be stored under optimum environmental conditions, given routine maintenance, and recopied every ten years. These steps should prevent the physical deterioration of the tapes, and the information they contain, until better media for long-term storage can be developed.

Figure 2: File Documentation

Background Information

File name: _____

Author of file: _____

Department: _____

Population or universe: _____

Geographic area: _____

Time frame: _____

Description of file contents: _____

Sampling and data collection procedures: _____

Hardware used to create the file: _____

Software used to create the file: _____

Types of output: _____

Citations: _____

Restrictions on use: _____

Technical Information

File location:　　Number of reels _____

　　　　　　　　Position of reel _____

File structure:　Rectangular _____

　　　　　　　　Hierarchical _____

Record Layout

Number of logical records: _____

Logical record types: Fixed-length_____

　　　　　　　　　　　Variable length_____

Logical record length: _____

Record size: _____ bytes

Block size: _____ bytes

For each field, specify:

Data element name	Field size	Starting position

Codebook

For each data element, specify:

Character type	Valid codes and their meaning

Conventions for missing or incorrect data:

The problem of hardware and software obsolescence is less acute now than it was several years ago. In general, most major computer manufacturers are now developing hardware and software to make their products "computer-friendly" as well as "user-friendly." Hardware designed to reduce computer incompatibility includes modems and specials diskdrives; software designed to reduce computer incompatibility includes telecommunication links and software utilities which can create uninterpreted data files or can translate data files into alternative codes. Uninterpreted data files can be used by a wider range of hardware and software configurations. Most data files requiring long-term preservation as machine-readable records can be converted to a format compatible with a range of hardware and software configurations, although the level of programming effort and cost may vary considerably. Obviously records created on hardware and software that are rapidly becoming obsolete should be converted to a format compatible with current technology as soon as possible.

Not all machine-readable records require long-term preservation as machine-readable records. The archival version of a large data file is generally the unaggregated microlevel master file—the file containing the most recent and correct version of the most discrete data file. Data summaries and abstracts are generally not saved since they can be generated again from the master file as required. Text files, graphics, and small database files are probably better preserved as hardcopies, either on acid-free paper or on computer output microfilm (COM).

Perfectly preserved machine-readable files lacking adequate documentation will be completely useless because it will be impossible to interpret the patterns of magnetic signals recorded. The documentation for machine-readable records destined for long-term storage should include the technical specifications for the file; a record layout describing the file structure; a codebook listing valid codes, their meanings, and conventions for missing data and unknown data; and any background information necessary for understanding the records (see Figure 2).

Transferring Machine-Readable Records to the Archives

Archivists decide whether to accept records based on their assessment of the future research potential of those records. In the case of machine-readable records, practical considerations such as the quality of a data file and its documentation, the type of storage medium, the degree of hardware and software dependence, and the archivist's familiarity with machine-readable records may also influence the decision whether or not to accept them.

Many archivists do not think automated data are records at all. Moreover, in a recent mail survey of 939 U. S. college and university archives, Stout and Baird (1984) found that only 69 universities (7.34%) reported any responsibility for machine-readable records. Even worse, two-thirds of the archivists who did accept machine-readable records reported that they had adopted no special measures for storing or maintaining these records, and that documentation was required for less than half of them.

Ideally, the anthropologist or archaeologist donating machine-readable records would begin to work with an archivist several years before the scheduled transfer of the records. Archivists accustomed to working with such records will be able to help the researcher at all stages of record transfer. If the archivist is not familiar with machine-readable records, however, more responsibility for ensuring their long-term preservation will fall to the researcher. Many archivists are not aware that arrangements can be made to store machine-readable records off-site at computer installations for a reasonable cost—often less than the cost of processing and storing a comparable volume of paper records. By contrast, many researchers will already have established a working relationship with the local computer facilities and will be knowledgeable about these arrangements. Archival processing of machine-readable records should include the creation of a new master copy and backup copy of each file, and adequate arrangements for their storage, maintenance, and distribution. Documentation should be checked for accuracy and completeness against a sample of the records.

If it appears that the archivist is unable to appreciate the value of important machine-readable records, or to store, maintain, and distribute them adequately, other arrangements should be made for their long-term care, and for the care of collections containing these records, since it is generally preferable to keep collections intact whenever possible.

Magnetic tape storage facility (Digital Electronic Corporation's Data Protection Service). Many computer installations now offer long-term archival storage for machine-readable records at a reasonable cost. (Courtesy of Professional Press)

CHAPTER 5. STORAGE
Mary Anne Kenworthy

Recommendations

The following general recommendations apply to all archival media; recommendations for storing specific media are described in the preceding chapters.

- Maintain temperature in the range of 60–75° F (16–24° C).
- Keep relative humidity between 40 and 50%.
- Make sure temperature and relative humidity are kept constant, as fluctuations are harmful and must be avoided.
- Monitor the storage environment, keeping records of temperature, relative humidity, and light levels.
- Protect all materials from sunlight and fluorescent light, using ultraviolet filter tubes or Plexiglas that filters ultraviolet rays.
- Construct shelving out of steel with a baked enamel finish or wood sealed with two to three coats of polyurethane varnish.
- Provide protection against fire and water damage throughout the storage area.
- Arrange for transfer of your records to an archives or other long-term storage facility.

Storage Considerations

The previous chapters have shown that, over time, all records and documents are subject to deterioration. The finest material and highest quality equipment are not enough to ensure the longevity of your records. The last and most crucial step in pre-

View of the field laboratory at the site of Quirigua, Guatemala, 1975. While environmental conditions often cannot be controlled during the course of research, they should be carefully monitored once the project returns from the field. (Courtesy of R. Sharer, The University Museum, University of Pennsylvania)

serving field records is to see that they are stored and cared for in a suitable environment. The following chapter will suggest guidelines for storing and housing the various kinds of records generated by anthropological/archaeological fieldwork.

The environment in which records are created, transported, and stored affects their life expectancy. Field conditions may not be predictable, but the environmental conditions in the office or research area should be controlled. The factors that most affect archival materials are temperature, relative humidity (RH), light, and air pollution. By storing materials at a constant temperature and RH, and by protecting them from light and physical damage, fragile documents can be preserved for many years.

J. Alden Mason in his office in the American Section, The University Museum, in the 1950s. The researcher's usual work space is not an archives, but steps can still be taken to protect valuable documents before they are moved to a long-term storage facility. (The University Museum, University of Pennsylvania)

Environmental Factors

The usual working area is not generally an archives. Several steps can nonetheless be taken to insure the longevity of records stored in offices. When records are not in use, they can be protected by folders and boxes preferably made of acid-free materials. If a project returns to the field for another season, let an air-conditioner maintain a constant temperature in the room where past seasons' records are stored.

The temperatures in storage areas should be kept as low as possible while maintaining a constant RH. Since storage areas are usually working areas, temperatures in the range of 60–75° F (16–24° C), provide a comfortable working environment. For every

18° F (10° C) rise in temperature, the rate of deterioration doubles for most archival material. The most damage done to collections is less likely to be the result of excessively high temperatures than of fluctuation or cycling of temperatures within the accepted ranges. A constant temperature should be maintained in the storage area.

The acceptable range for RH is between 40 and 50%. When materials are stored in an environment of 40% RH or less, paper becomes brittle and photographic emulsions may crack. An environment of greater than 50% RH, on the other hand, promotes fungus and mold growth. These organisms weaken and stain paper permanently and soften photographic emulsions so that they become sticky. Sometimes fungus and mold growth is fostered by the existence of microenvironments within the storage area. Small spaces will develop different temperatures and RH if the air becomes stagnant and is not able to circulate freely. A good air ventilation system helps prevent the formation of microenvironments. It is important to remember that changes in temperature also proportionately affect the relative humidity. The higher the ambient temperature, the greater the amount of water vapor the air is capable of holding, and the higher the relative humidity.

Ultraviolet light and visible light both have debilitating effects on paper and photographs. They fade and bleach papers and inks, obliterating valuable information. Archival material should never be exposed to sunlight or fluorescent light. Documents can be protected from the harmful effects of light by boxing and storing papers on shelves or in filing cabinets. Papers and photographs should not be left on tables near windows, nor should they remain on tabletops for long periods of time.

Air pollution is detrimental to all archival records. In urban areas it is almost impossible to avoid the effects of gaseous pollutants. Material can, however, be protected from everyday dirt and dust. Routine housecleaning will prevent dirt from accumulating and causing physical damage.

Smoking and drinking should not be allowed among the records. Cigarettes emit smoke that yellows both papers and photographs, and they also represent a fire hazard. Crumbs will attract rodents and insects that will feed on paper, photograpic emulsions, and magnetic tapes. Drinks will spill, staining papers indelibly and destroying tapes and negatives.

The effect of mold and fungus growth on photographs. Simple precautions and careful monitoring of the environment can help prevent such disasters. (The University Museum, University of Pennsylvania)

Monitoring

For long-term storage considerations, a careful monitoring system is essential. A monitoring system gives a daily record of temperature and RH in the storage area. This record will serve as a guide to maintain control over the entire collection. A daily record of temperature and humidity fluctuations will alert you to any potential problems. For example, high humidity caused by a leak in the ceiling of the storage area will be obvious if a daily chart is kept. Cycling of the environment, daily fluctuations in temperature and RH, should be avoided as much as possible. Although environmental monitoring can be very expensive, there are several economical methods for ensuring adequate environmental control of storage areas.

Temperature can be monitored by placing a thermometer at strategic spots in the storage area. RH indicator cards are an inexpensive means of determining the relative humidity in a room; the cards change color according to the amount of moisture present in the atmosphere. The indicators are calibrated to be accurate to within a range of 5%. More precise measures are provided by a recording hygrothermograph, an instrument designed to measure precisely the temperature and relative humidity of a room and record the data on a chart. It gives a constant reading of the temperature and relative humidity over a 24-hour period. Daily, weekly, and monthly cycling are easily interpreted when using a hygrothermograph. Another instrument that measures the relative humidity in an area is the sling psychrometer, which calculates the humidity using two internal thermometers. The reading is less accurate than the hygrothermograph as the psychrometer must be manually operated, but the latter is the less expensive of the two instruments.

As mentioned before, direct sunlight and fluorescent light should be avoided in the storage area. Plexiglas filters will cover windows and prevent the damaging rays from entering. Ultraviolet filtering sleeves are also available to cover fluorescent tubes. Light levels should be kept as low as possible in the storage area, within the range of 5–15 footcandles. An inexpensive way to monitor the intensity of light is to use a photographic light meter. Using a Weston Ranger 9 photographic light meter, for instance, a reading of 9 on the meter is equivalent to 2 footcandles. A reading of 12 on the same meter corresponds to approximately 16 footcandles. Each commercial meter supplies its own conversion chart from light level readings to footcandles.

Monitoring air quality is more difficult since it involves very expensive equipment. Charcoal filters will remove gaseous pollutants from the air and fiberglass filters will remove solid particles. Ideally, these filtration systems should be incorporated in the heating and cooling systems of the building where the storage area is located.

Collections should be protected against the possibility of water and fire damage. Halon, short for halogenated hydrocarbon, is a gas that interferes with the combustion cycle to suppress a fire. This system is recommended in museums and archives since it does not damage collections. The Halon fire suppression system is expensive to install and maintain, however, and is effective

The stained, faded, and mildewed notebooks at the top of the photograph were damaged in a basement flood, whereas the charred and brittle letters on the bottom were the victims of a laboratory fire. (The University Museum, University of Pennsylvania)

only in small rooms and only for several minutes. A Halon system will not protect against deep-seated fires that may work their way into storage containers. Water sprinkler systems operate by sensing a change in the room temperature. Each sprinkler head has its own sensing device and operates independently. Water damage is an important consideration if a sprinkler system is installed, but not an excuse to be without a fire suppression system. For smaller areas and budgets, smoke detectors and portable fire extinguishers provide excellent protection in case of an emergency. Halon is available in portable fire extinguishers, but any extinguisher that is effective against paper, chemical, or electrical fires is recommended.

If the storage area is located in a basement where there is a real possibility of flooding, an inexpensive water detection system should be installed. Papers can be protected from the danger of flooding by placing record boxes on platforms above the floor. If exposed pipes traverse the storage area, plastic dropcloths should be kept nearby in case of leakage.

Fire detection and suppression systems and water detection systems should be installed and monitored with the help and co-operation of the security and building management. The local fire department can help in specifying the regulations and local ordinances applying to the storage area. People working with the material should be aware of the systems protecting the collection and how to act in a time of emergency.

Housing

A massive amount of documentation will accrue for field projects lasting several years or even decades. All projects demand an organized storage system to protect material from physical and mechanical damage. The following guidelines should help you decide on supplies and spatial divisions.

All shelving and storage units should be constructed of steel coated with a baked enamel finish. If existing furniture in the room is constructed of wood, this furniture may be used IF it is thoroughly coated with several layers of polyurethane varnish. Unsealed wood, due to its inherent acidity, should never come in contact with paper or photographs.

Improper storage of oversize documents. These maps and drawings should not be stored loosely rolled and upright, but rather laid out flat in a map case, or rolled around a pH neutral tube that is then stored horizontally. (The University Museum, University of Pennsylvania)

Oversized material such as maps, architectural drawings and blueprints should be placed in acid-free folders, approximately the same size as the material itself, and stored in special map cases. The latter should be constructed of the same steel with enamel finish as all other storage equipment and should have drawers two inches thick or less. This arrangement allows for the largest amount of drawer space while protecting the individual maps from being too tightly stacked on top of one another.

If a record is too large for storage in a map case, it may be rolled around the outside of a neutral pH tube. Between the record and the tube a sheet of acid-free paper should be rolled. A sheet of acid-free paper is also used to protect the outside of the oversize document. The tubes can then be labelled and stored horizontally across the top of the map case or in some other suitable space. The tubes should not be stored vertically.

Proper storage of documents. Acid-free folders and boxes provide the best protection for important records. (The University Museum, University of Pennsylvania)

Folders and boxes for individual papers and books should be acid-free, with a pH of 7, or more. Loose unbound paper records should be stored in acid-free folders and placed in neutral boxes. Photographic materials should be stored exclusively in neutral, pH 7, folders. There is evidence that buffered storage supplies increase the rate of yellowing in albumen prints. For this reason, and until more research is conducted, it is probably better to store all photographic material in neutral enclosures. Photographic negatives and prints should be housed separately and stored in individual enclosures.

Inert, chemically stable polyester film such as Mylar D (Dupont) is also an acceptable storage material for paper and photographs. The question of paper versus plastic enclosures is a matter of cost versus preference. Paper enclosures are less expensive to purchase and are opaque; they will protect the material from light exposure. Documents and photographs stored in plastic enclosures, however, are immediately visible, and the chance of damage from excessive and careless handling is greatly reduced. The print does not have to be removed from its envelope to be viewed as it does in the case of paper enclosures. Unfortunately, inert polyester materials cost more than paper.

Storage containers, buffered or non-buffered, are available in every imaginable size and format. Be wary of suppliers who sell so-called "archival" material as well as huge stocks of other supplies. There is one simple method to test supplies. A pH testing pen is available for a few dollars and will immediately indicate the acidity of the material. Supplies should be checked to see if they conform to archival standards and returned to the manufacturer if they do not.

Both the Society of American Archivists (SAA) and the American National Standards Institute (ANSI) specify recomendations for archival enclosures for papers and photographs. ANSI also specifies storage conditions for both types of documents, as well as for other media such as microfilm and audiotape. Researchers are encouraged to consult the ANSI standards and other literature listed in the bibliography for national guidelines. If these standards are considered during the research phase, conservation problems will not arise at a later date.

After they have been published, your records should be stored permanently in an archives to save office space and provide them with a suitable environment. Several factors should be considered when selecting an appropriate repository. What are the scope and existing holdings of the archives under consideration? Will your records complement the holdings in the archives, or will they become an ill-used eccentricity unavailable to other scholars and the public? Finally, does the potential repository have the storage space, staff, and time to process the records? The collection should not only be made available to the wider research community, but this process should occur in a reasonable amount of time. Institutions that collect records such as the American Philosophical Society and the National Anthropological Archives at the Smithsonian Institution will be happy to supply guidelines for donations. In addition, researchers can supply some rules of their own. Papers most often may be donated with restrictions regarding copyright and privacy.

View of The University Museum Archives, University of Pennsylvania. (Courtesy of M. Wakely, Philadelphia, Pennsylvania)

As noted in all the previous chapters of the Manual, if proper care is taken with documents in all stages of a project, from planning to final publication, the information will never be lost. If thought is given throughout the duration of a project to the quality of supplies, the handling of the documents, and the short- and long-term storage of materials, the record of the research will remain intact long after the work has ended.

Dennis Jones writing notes after a day of surveying at the site of El Mirador, Guatemala, 1982. (Courtesy of Mark Philbrick, Brigham Young University Public Communications)

TIME LINE
FOR RECORD PRESERVATION

compiled by
Eleanor M. King

STAGES	STEPS TOWARDS RECORD PRESERVATION
formulating research	• assess archival importance of project • determine which records will best document each stage
writing proposal	• budget for preservation of important records • consider choices such as documenting in black and white as well as color film, and using carbon typewriter ribbon or soft pencil rather than ink for writing permanent records

PROJECT BEGINS
(PLANNING)

	supply storage	• keep paper, film, and magnetic tapes or disks in dustproof, waterproof, and insectproof containers, preferably metal • store all media in a dark, cool, dry environment; take measures to control fluctuations in temperature and humidity like storing materials in an air conditioned room, or adding silica gel to storage containers where the climate is very humid
PROJECT IN FIELD	supply use	• clean equipment (cameras, tape recorders, computers) regularly • make sure supplies and equipment are at the same ambient temperature when used (*e.q.*, film and camera) • do not leave equipment in sun, or small enclosed spaces (glove compartments, car trunks), especially when loaded and in use • protect magnetic media from magnetic fields
	care of new documents	• once a document is produced, do not secure with adhesives and steel staples • make sure all important machine-readable files are write-protected unless being updated; create a duplicate before updating • inspect records carefully prior to leaving the field to make sure they have not been harmed by destructive insects or fungi; clean or fumigate them before shipping home if problem organisms are found

PROJECT RETURNS
(DATA ANALYSIS)

long-term document
storage

- create an optimum storage area for all media
- keep important paper records in acid-free files and boxes in long-term storage if not frequently in use
- copy motion picture film onto cartridge format and make separate copies of magnetic motion picture soundtracks to store with other magnetic media
- prepare master copies of important photographic materials, machine-readable files, and cassette or video tapes to place in optimum storage; use duplicates for daily work
- update stored files regularly; new files generated by data analysis should be duplicated, and one copy placed in optimum storage
- keep a log on physical condition of each stored document; the log may also serve as a storage inventory

short-term document
storage

- keep important records in one place and control loans out
- protect working documents from air pollution and dust by storing in appropriate containers
- avoid extremes and fluctuations in the ambient temperature and humidity of working areas as much as possible
- handle all original records carefully; use cotton gloves when working with magnetic tapes or film; avoid bending or folding documents

PROJECT CONTINUES (PUBLICATION)

every year
- rewind all stored magnetic tapes (sound, video, computer) to prevent print- or bleed-through
- check alignment of working tapes for proper tension
- make sure the information on machine-readable master records is up-to-date and complete
- check environmental conditions in long-term storage area to make sure they are still optimal; also check monitoring devices to ensure they are working properly
- inventory important documents to confirm their wheareabouts

every 2–3 years
- recopy floppy and flexible disks

every 5–10 years
- check important paper records for signs of wear, tear, and surface dirt; photocopy, mend, and/or clean deteriorating documents
- inventory master negatives, slides, and prints for signs of deterioration; replace damaged ones
- recopy master magnetic tapes
- make sure master machine-readable records are still compatible with currently available hardware and software; transfer or copy obsolescent or unused ones onto magnetic tape
- remember to update master log on physical condition of stored records

every 10–20 years
- replace master magnetic tapes

PROJECT ENDS

planning for permanent
storage

- choose in advance an appropriate repository for project records
- donate records in bulk, once
project has ended, not piece-
meal
- discuss the terms of transfer
with the archivist or records-
keeper in charge of the repository ahead of time; be sure any
restrictions on use are written
into the deed of gift

transferring records
to permanent storage

- copy permanent records
stored on magnetic disks onto
magnetic tape prior to transfer
- make sure all records are accurately and legibly labelled
before transferring them;
paper records should be legibly written
- provide repository staff with
adequate documentation on
how records were created
- write a brief overview ex-
plaining the project to the repository staff; include dates,
sponsors, project goals, per-
sonnel, and research accom-
plishments, such as significant
findings and publications

BIBLIOGRAPHY

General

American National Standards Institute. For a list of ANSI literature, write to: American National Standards Institute, 1430 Broadway, New York, NY 10018. [Also see individual listings under chapter bibliographies.]

Baker, John P., and Marguerite C. Soroka, eds. 1978. *Library Conservation: Preservation in Perspective.* Stroudsburg, PA: Dowden, Hutchinson and Ross.

Cunha, George M. 1975. Conserving Local Archival Materials on a Limited Budget. Technical Leaflet No. 86. *History News* (Nov.). Nashville, TN: American Association for State and Local History.

Cunha, George M., and Dorothy Grant Cunha. 1971. *Conservation of Library Materials: A Manual and Bibliography on the Care, Repair, and Restoration of Library Materials,* Vol. 1. 2d ed. Metuchen, NJ: Scarecrow Press.

Cunha, George M., and Dorothy Grant Cunha. 1972. *Library and Archives Conservation: 1980's and Beyond.* Metuchen, NJ: Scarecrow Press.

History News. Features articles on preservation and conservation of documents, as well as periodic Technical Leaflets on the same issues. Published by the American Association for State and Local History, 708 Berry Rd., Nashville, TN 37204.

Library of Congress. *Preservation Leaflets.* For a list of available pamphlets, write to the Library of Congress, Washington, DC. [Also see individual listings under chapter bibliographies.]

Ritzenthaler, Mary Lynn. 1983. *Archives & Manuscripts: Conservation. A Manual on Physical Care and Management.* SAA Basic Manual Series. Chicago: Society of American Archivists. [Deals mostly with paper, but contains useful general guidelines and an extensive annotated bibliography for all media.]

Society of American Archivists (SAA) Basic Manual Series. For a list of publications, write to: SAA, 330 S. Wells, Suite 810, Chicago, IL 60606. [Also see individual listings under chapter bibliographies.]

Swartzburg, Susan G. 1980. *Preserving Library Materials.* Metuchen, NJ: Scarecrow Press.

Swartzburg, Susan G., ed. 1983. *Conservation in the Library. A Handbook of Use and Care of Traditional and Nontraditional Materials.* Westport, CN: Greenwood Press.

Willson, Nancy, ed. 1979. *Museum and Archival Supplies Handbook.* 2d ed. Toronto: Ontario Museum Association and the Toronto Area Archivists' Group.

Preservation of Paper Records

American National Standards Institute. 1974. *Methylene Blue Method for Measuring Thiosulfate and Silver Densitometric Method for Measuring Residue Chemicals in Films, Plates, and Papers.* New York: ANSI.

American Society for Testing and Materials. 1976. *Standard Specification for Bond and Ledger Papers for Permanent Records.* Philadelphia: ASTM.

American Society for Testing and Materials. 1976. *Standard Specification for File Folders for Storage of Permanent Records.* Philadelphia: ASTM.

Baer, N. S., N. Indictor, and W. H. Phelan. 1971. An Evaluation of Adhesives for Use in Paper Conservation. *Guild of Book Workers Journal* 10(1):36–38.

Barrow, W. J. 1953. Migration of Impurities in Paper. *Archivum* 3:105–108.

Barrow, W. J., Research Laboratory. 1964a. *Test Data of Naturally Aged Papers.* Permanence/Durability of the Book No. 2. Richmond, VA: W. J. Barrow Research Laboratory.

Barrow, W. J., Research Laboratory. 1964b. *Spray Deacidification.* Permanence/Durability of the Book No. 3. Richmond, VA: W. J. Barrow Research Laboratory.

Barrow, W. J., Research Laboratory. 1969. *Spot Testing for Unstable Modern Book and Record Papers.* Permanence/Durability of the Book No. 6. Richmond, VA: W. J. Barrow Research Laboratory.

Barrow, W. J., Research Laboratory. 1974. *Physical and Chemical Properties of Book Papers, 1507–1949.* Permanence/Durability of the Book No. 7. Richmond, VA: W. J. Barrow Research Laboratory. [Other literature on book paper and its conservation available from the same source, in the Permanence/Durability of the Book series.]

Brown, Margaret R. 1982. *Boxes for the Protection of Rare Books: Their Design and Construction.* Washington, DC: Preservation Office, Library of Congress.

Bureau, William H. 1972. *Understanding Paper Properties, Parts I–IV. Graphics Arts Monthly* 45(3,5,6,7).

Daniels, V. 1979. Air Pollution and the Archivist. *Journal of the Society of Archivists* 6:154–156.

Gilbert, Edward R. 1982. A Conservation Primer: The Preservation of Library Materials in Tropical Climates. *Bulletin of the Florida Chapter, Special Libraries Association* 14:110–127.

Harris, Carolyn. 1979. Mass Deacidification: Science to the Rescue? *Library Journal* 104(July):1423–1427.

Heim, Roger, Francoise Flieder, and Jacqueline Nicot. 1968. Combatting the Moulds which Develop on Cultural Property in Tropical Climates. *The Conservation of Cultural Property with Special Reference to Tropical Conditions.* Paris: UNESCO.

Hunter, Dard. 1978 (1943). *Papermaking: The History and Technique of an Ancient Craft.* 3d ed. New York: Dover Press.

Kyle, Hedi. 1983. *Library Materials Preservation Manual. Practical Methods for Preserving Books, Pamphlets and Other Printed Materials.* Bronxville, NY: Nicholas T. Smith.

Launer, Herbert F., and William K. Wilson. 1947. Photochemical Stability of Papers. *Journal of Research of the Bureau of Standards* 30:55–74.

Library of Congress. 1975. *Selected References in the Literature of Conservation.* Washington, DC: Library of Congress.

Library of Congress. 1975. *Preserving Newspapers and Newspaper-Type Materials.* Washington, DC: Library of Congress.

Library of Congress. 1980. *Polyester Film Encapsulation.* Washington, DC: Library of Congress.

Meynell, G. G. and R. J. Newsam. 1978. Foxing, a Fungal Infection of Paper. *Nature* 274:466–468.

Mitchell, Charles A., and Thomas C. Hepworth. 1937. *Inks, Their Composition and Manufacture.* London: Griffin and Company, Ltd.

Morrow, Carolyn Clark. 1982. *Conservation Treatment Procedures: A Manual for Step-by-Step Procedures for the Maintenance and Repair of Library Materials.* Littleton, CO: Libraries Unlimited, Inc.

National Conservation Advisory Council. 1980. *Conservation Treatment Facilities in the United States.* Washington, DC: National Conservation Advisory Council.

Parks, E. J., and W. K. Wilson. 1974. *Evaluation of Archival Stability of Copies from Representative Office Copying Machines.* Washington, DC: National Bureau of Standards.

Ritzenthaler, Mary Lynn. 1983. *Archives & Manuscripts: Conservation. A Manual on Physical Care and Management.* SAA Basic Manual Series. Chicago: Society of American Archivists.

Smith, Merrily A., Norvell M. M. Jones, II, Susan L. Page, and Marian Peck Dirda. 1984. Pressure-Sensitive Tape and Techniques for Its Removal from Paper. *Journal of the American Institute for Conservation* 23:101–113.

Trinkhaus-Randall, Gregor. 1980. Effects of the Environment on Paper: A Review of Recent Literature. Technical Leaflet No. 128. *History News* (July). Nashville, TN: American Association for State and Local History.

Warren, S. D., Company. 1981. *Paper Permanence: Preserving the Written Word.* Boston: Scott Paper Company.

Wink, W. A. 1961. The Effect of Relative Humidity and Temperature on Paper Properties. *Technical Association of the Pulp and Paper Industry* 44:171A–180A. Atlanta, GA.

Film, Tape and Video

American National Standards Institute. 1974. *Method for Evaluating the Processing for Black and White Photographic Papers with Respect to the Stability of the Resultant Image* (PH 4.32-1974). New York: ANSI.

American National Standards Institute. 1976. *Specifications for Photographic Films for Archival Records, Silver-Gelatin Type, on Polyester Base* (PH 1.41-1976). New York: ANSI.

American National Standards Institute. 1978. *Requirements for Photographic Filing Enclosures for Storing Processed Photographic Films, Plates and Papers* (PH 1.53-1978). New York: ANSI.

Balsley, G., and P. Moore. 1980. How to File and Store Slides. *Modern Photography* (Jan.).

Barrett, R. 1982. Developments in Optical Disk Technology and the Implications for Information Storage and Retrieval. *Journal of Micrographics* 15(1):22–26.

Eastman Kodak Company. 1973. *Black/White Processing for Permanence.* Kodak Publication No. J-19. Rochester, NY: Eastman Kodak Company.

Eastman Kodak Company. 1978. *Notes on Tropical Photography.* Kodak Publication No. C-24. Rochester, NY: Eastman Kodak Company.

Eastman Kodak Company. 1979. *Preservation of Photographs.* Kodak Publication No. F-30. Rochester, NY: Eastman Kodak Company.

Eastman Kodak Company. 1981. *Storage and Preservation of Microfilms.* Kodak Publication No. D-31. Rochester, NY: Eastman Kodak Company.

Eastman Kodak Company. 1985. *Conservation of Photographs.* Kodak Publication No. F-40. Rochester, NY: Eastman Kodak Company. [Supersedes No. F-30, *Preservation of Photographs.*]

Eaton, G. T. 1970. Preservation, Deterioration and Restoration of Photographic Images. *Library Quarterly* 40(1):85–98.

Hendriks, Klaus B. 1982. The Conservation of Photographic Materials. *Picturescope* 30(1):4–11.

Kach, David. 1978. Photographic Dilemma: Stability of Storage of Color Materials. *Industrial Photography* 27:8–28.

Keefe, Laurence E., Jr., and Dennis Inch. 1984. *The Life of a Photograph.* Boston: Focal Press.

Materazzi, Albert R. 1978. Archival Stability of Microfilm—A Technical Review. *Technical Report* No. 18, August 4. Washington, DC: U.S. Government Printing Office.

McWilliams, Jerry. 1979. *The Preservation and Restoration of Sound Recordings.* Nashville, TN: American Association for State and Local History.

Nghiep Cong Bui, Dominic. 1984. The Videodisk: Technology, Applications, and Some Implications for Archives. *The American Archivist* 47(4):418–427.

Noble, Richard. 1980. Archival Preservation of Motion Pictures: A Summary of Current Findings. Technical Leaflet No. 3126. *History News* (April). Nashville, TN: American Association for State and Local History.

Ostroff, Eugene. 1976. *Conserving and Restoring Photographic Collections.* Washington, DC: American Association of Museums.

Ostroff, Eugene. 1967. Preservation of Photographs. *Photographic Journal* 107:309–314.

Photographic Conservation. Published by the Graphic Arts Research Center, Rochester Institute of Technology, One Lomb Memorial Drive, Rochester, NY 14623.

Picturescope. Features articles on conservation and preservation of photographs. Published as the Quarterly Bulletin of the Picture Division, Special Libraries Association, P.O. Box 50119, F Street Station, Tariff Commission Building, Washington, DC 20004.

Rempel, Siegfried. n.d. The Care of Black and White Photographic Collections: Identification of Processes. *Technical Bulletin* No. 6. Ottawa, Ontario: Canadian Conservation Institute of the National Museums of Canada.

Ritzenthaler, Mary Lynn, Gerald J. Munoff, and Margery S. Long. 1984. *Archives & Manuscripts: Administration of Photographic Collections.* SAA Basic Manual Series. Chicago: Society of American Archivists.

Sargent, Ralph N. 1974. *The Preservation of Moving Images.* Corporation for Public Broadcasting and National Endowment for the Arts.

Short, J. Michael. 1982. Photographic Preservation for the Archaeologist. *Northwest Anthropological Research Notes* 16(Fall):212–220. [Useful specific details on materials and methods.]

Sirkin, Arlene F. 1980. The Videodisc Revolution. *Picturescope* 28(3):1,29–30.

Suthasinekul, S. 1980. Microfilm Versus Optical Disk as a Storage Medium for Document-Retrieval and Dissemination. *Journal of ASIS* 17(3):100–102.

Swartzburg, Susan G. 1980. *Preserving Library Materials.* Metuchen, NJ: Scarecrow Press.

Swartzburg, Susan G., and Deirdre Boyle. 1983. Videotape. In *Conservation in the Library. A Handbook of Use and Care of Traditional and Nontraditional Materials,* ed. S. G. Swartzburg, 155–162. Westport, CN: Greenwood Press.

Weinstein, Robert A., and Larry Booth. 1977. *Collection, Use, and Care of Historical Photographs.* Nashville, TN: American Association for State and Local History.

Wilhelm, Henry. 1970. *Procedures for Processing and Storing Black-and-White Photographs for Maximum Possible Permanence.* Grinnell, Iowa: East Street Gallery.

Wilhelm, Henry. 1979. Color Print Instability. *Modern Photography* (Feb.).

Wilhelm, Henry. 1982. Problems with Long-term Stability of Kodak Professional Direct Duplicating Film. *Picturescope* 30(1):24–33.

Machine-Readable Records

Bell, Lionel. 1976. *The Archival Implications of Machine-Readable Records.* Washington, DC: International Congress on Archives.

Bell, Lionel. 1979. The Archival Implications of Machine-Readable Records. *Archivum* 26(1):85–92.

Bisco, Ralph, ed. 1969. *Data Bases, Computers, and the Social Sciences.* New York: John Wiley and Sons.

Carroll, M. E. 1976. A Perspective on Machine-Readable Archives and Public Service. *Automatic Data Processing in Archives* 2(1):7–10.

Clark, B. M. 1983. Social Science Data Archives and Libraries. *Library Trends* 31(3):505–509.

Dollar, C. M. 1978. Appraising Machine-Readable Records. *The American Archivist* 41:423–430.

Fischbein, Meyer H. 1980. *Guidelines for Administering Machine-Readable Records.* Washington, DC: Automatic Data Processing Committee of the International Council on Archives.

Geda, Carolyn L., Erik W. Austin, and Francis X. Blouin, Jr., eds. 1980. *Archives and Machine-Readable Records.* Chicago: Society of American Archivists.

Geller, Sidney B. 1974. Archival Data Storage. *Datamation* 20(10):72–80.

Geller, Sidney B. 1976. Erasing Myths About Magnetic Media. *Datamation* 22(3):65–68.

Ham, David, *et al.* 1981. *Archival Preservation of Machine-Readable Records: A Final Report of the Wisconsin Survey of Machine-Readable Public Records.* Madison, WI: State Historical Society.

Geller, Sidney B. 1983. *Care and Handling of Computer Magnetic Storage Media.* Washington, DC: U.S. Department of Commerce, National Bureau of Standards.

Hedstrom, Margaret L. 1981. Computers, Privacy, and Research Access to Confidential Information. *The Midwestern Archivist* 6(1).

Hedstrom, Margaret L. 1984. *Machine-Readable Records.* Chicago: Society of American Archivists.

King, Harold, and Mitchell Krasny. 1975. A Standard Description for Magnetic Tape Files. *Annals of Economic and Social Measurement* 4(3):449–454.

Klein, R. G., and K. Cruz-Uribe. 1984. *The Analysis of Animal Bones from Archaeological Sites.* Chicago: University of Chicago Press.

Lancaster, Wilfred F. 1979. *Information Retrieval Systems: Characteristics, Testing, and Evaluation.* New York: John Wiley and Sons.

Lowell, Howard P. 1982. Preserving Recorded Information. *Records Management Quarterly* 16(2):38–42.

Martin, David, and Gerald Ham, *et al. Archival Preservation of Machine-Readable Records: Final Report of the Wisconsin Survey of Machine-Readable Records.* Madison: State Historical Society of Wisconsin.

Mihran, Danielle, and G. Arthur Mihran. 1981. On Structuring the Archival Repository for Scientists' Machine-Readable Records. *Proceedings of ASIS* 18:182–183.

National Archives and Record Service. 1975. *Computer Output Microfilm.* Washington, DC: U.S. Government Printing Office.

Robbin, Alice. 1979. Understanding the Machine-Readable Numeric Record: Archival Challenges with Some Comments on Appraisal Guidelines. *The Midwestern Archivist* 6(1):5–24.

Roper, Michael. 1982. Advanced Technical Media: The Conservation and Storage of Audio-Visual and Machine-Readable Records. *Journal of the Society of Archivists* 7(2):106–112.

Stout, Leo J., and Donald A. Baird. 1984. Automation in North American College and University Archives: A Survey. *The American Archivist* 47(4):394–404.

Thibodeau, Kenneth. 1976. Machine-Readable Archives and Future History. *Computers and the Humanities* 10(2):89–92.

U.S. General Services Administration, National Archives and Records Service, Data Archives Branch. 1972. *Handbook of Recommended Environmental Conditions and Handling Procedures for Magnetic Tape.* Washington, DC: U.S. Government Printing Office.

Storage

Baas, Valerie. 1980. Know Your Enemies. *History News* 35:40–41.

Banks, Paul N. 1974. Environmental Standards for Storage of Books and Manuscripts. *Library Journal* 99:339–343.

Bohem, Hilda. 1978 (April). *Disaster Prevention and Disaster Preparedness.* Berkeley: Office of the Assistant Vice President—Library Plans and Policies, Systemwide Administration, University of California.

Brommelle, Norman S., and J. B. Harris. 1962. Aspects of the Effect of Light on Deterioration. *Museum News* 62:337–346.

Buck, R. D. 1964. A Specification for Museum Air Conditioning. *Museum News,* Technical Supplement No. 6, 43(4).

Clapp, Anne F. 1978. *Curatorial Care of Works of Art on Paper.* 3d ed. Oberlin: Intermuseum Conservation Association.

Cunha, George M., and Dorothy Grant Cunha. 1971. *Conservation of Library Materials: A Manual and Bibliography on the Care, Repair and Restoration of Library Materials,* Vol. 1, 2d ed. Metuchen, NJ: Scarecrow Press.

Edwards, Stephen R., Bruce M. Bell, and Mary Elizabeth King, comps. 1981. *Pest Control in Museums: A Status Report (1980).* Lawrence, KS: Association of Systematics Collections.

Feller, R. L. 1964. Control of Deteriorating Effects of Light on Museum Objects. *Museum News* 17:39–47.

General Services Administration. Public Building Service. 1977 (April). *Protecting Records Centers and Archives from Fire: Report of the General Services Administration Advisory Committee on the Protection of Archives and Records Centers.* Washington, DC: U.S. Government Printing Office.

International Council of Museums. 1969. *Products and Instruments Suitable for Use in Museums for Protection Against Damage by Light.* Lighting Group, Draft Number 2.

LaFontaine, R. H. 1980. *Recommended Environmental Monitors for Museums, Archives, and Art Galleries.* Ottawa, Ontario: CCI Technical Bulletin 3.

MacLeod, K. J. 1978a. *Museum Lighting.* Ottawa, Ontario: Canadian Conservation Institute.

MacLeod, K. J. 1978b. *Relative Humidity: Its Importance, Measurement, and Control in Museums.* Ottawa, Ontario: CCI Technical Bulletin 1.

Mason, Philip P. 1975 (Oct.). Archival Security: New Solutions to an Old Problem. *The American Archivist* 38:477–492.

National Fire Protection Association. 1980. *Archives and Records Centers. NFPA 232 AM.* Boston: National Fire Protection Association.

Ritzenthaler, Mary Lynn. 1983. *Archives & Manuscripts: Conservation. A Manual on Physical Care and Management.* SAA Basic Manual Series. Chicago: Society of American Archivists.

Szent-Ivany, J. J. H. 1968. Identification and Control of Insect Pests. *The Conservation of Cultural Property with Special Reference to Tropical Conditions.* Paris: UNESCO.

Thomson, G. 1978. *The Museum Environment.* London: Butterworth.

Trinkhaus-Randall, Gregor. 1980. Effects of the Environment on Paper: A Review of Recent Literature. Technical Leaflet No. 128. *History News* (July). Nashville, TN: American Association for State and Local History.

Walch, Timothy. 1977. *Archives & Manuscripts: Security.* SAA Basic Manual Series. Chicago: Society of American Archivists.

Wessel, Carl J. 1972. Deterioration of Library Materials. *Encyclopedia of Library and Information Science*, Vol. 7. New York: Marcel Dekker, Inc.

Willson, N., ed. 1979. *Museum and Archival Supplies Handbook.* 2d ed. Toronto, Ontario: Ontario Museum Association and Toronto Area Archivists Group.